HAGERSTOWN-JEFFERSON TWP PUBLIC LIBRARY

3 9213 00061893 8

W9-AUY-212

Robert
Downey Jr.

Other titles in the People in the News series include:

Maya Angelou	Coretta Scott King
Tyra Banks	Ashton Kutcher
David Beckham	Tobey Maguire
Beyoncé	Eli Manning
Fidel Castro	John McCain
Kelly Clarkson	Barak Obama
Hillary Clinton	Michelle Obama
Miley Cyrus	Danica Patrick
Ellen Degeneres	Nancy Pelosi
Hilary Duff	Queen Latifah
Zac Efron	Daniel Radcliffe
Brett Favre	Condoleezza Rice
50 Cent	Rihanna
Al Gore	J.K. Rowling
Tony Hawk	Shakira
Salma Hayek	Tupac Shakur
LeBron James	Will Smith
Jay-Z	Gwen Stefani
Derek Jeter	Ben Stiller
Steve Jobs	Hilary Swank
Dwayne Johnson	Justin Timberlake
Angelina Jolie	Usher
Jonas Brothers	Denzel Washington
Kim Jong Il	Oprah Winfrey

Robert Downey Jr.

by Laurie Collier Hillstrom

Property of
Hagerstown-Jefferson Twp
Public Library

LUCENT BOOKS
A part of Gale, Cengage Learning

GALE
CENGAGE Learning

Detroit • New York • San Francisco • New Haven, Conn • Waterville, Maine • London

GALE
CENGAGE Learning·

© 2011 Gale, Cengage Learning

ALL RIGHTS RESERVED. No part of this work covered by the copyright herein may be reproduced, transmitted, stored, or used in any form or by any means graphic, electronic, or mechanical, including but not limited to photocopying, recording, scanning, digitizing, taping, Web distribution, information networks, or information storage and retrieval systems, except as permitted under Section 107 or 108 of the 1976 United States Copyright Act, without the prior written permission of the publisher.

Every effort has been made to trace the owners of copyrighted material.

LIBRARY OF CONGRESS CATALOGING-IN-PUBLICATION DATA

Hillstrom, Laurie Collier, 1965-
 Robert Downey Jr. / by Laurie Collier Hillstrom.
  p. cm. -- (People in the news)
 Includes bibliographical references and index.
 ISBN 978-1-4205-0569-6 (hardcover)
 1. Downey, Robert, 1965- Juvenile literature. 2. Actors--United States--Biography--Juvenile literature. I. Title.
 PN2287.D548H55 2011
 791.430'28092--dc22
 [B]
                                                          2010042125

Lucent Books
27500 Drake Rd.
Farmington Hills, MI 48331

ISBN-13: 978-1-4205-0569-6
ISBN-10: 1-4205-0569-6

Printed in the United States of America
1 2 3 4 5 6 7 15 14 13 12 11

Printed by Bang Printing, Brainerd, MN, 1st Ptg., 03/2011

Contents

ame and celebrity are alluring. People are drawn to those who walk in fame's spotlight, whether they are known for great accomplishments or for notorious deeds. The lives of the famous pique public interest and attract attention, perhaps because their experiences seem in some ways so different from, yet in other ways so similar to, our own.

Newspapers, magazines, and television regularly capitalize on this fascination with celebrity by running profiles of famous people. For example, television programs such as *Entertainment Tonight* devote all of their programming to stories about entertainment and entertainers. Magazines such as *People* fill their pages with stories of the private lives of famous people. Even newspapers, newsmagazines, and television news frequently delve into the lives of well-known personalities. Despite the number of articles and programs, few provide more than a superficial glimpse at their subjects.

Lucent's People in the News series offers young readers a deeper look into the lives of today's newsmakers, the influences that have shaped them, and the impact they have had in their fields of endeavor and on other people's lives. The subjects of the series hail from many disciplines and walks of life. They include authors, musicians, athletes, political leaders, entertainers, entrepreneurs, and others who have made a mark on modern life and who, in many cases, will continue to do so for years to come.

These biographies are more than factual chronicles. Each book emphasizes the contributions, accomplishments, or deeds that have brought fame or notoriety to the individual and shows how that person has influenced modern life. Authors portray their subjects in a realistic, unsentimental light. For example, Bill Gates—the cofounder and chief executive officer of the software giant Microsoft—has been instrumental in making personal computers the most vital tool of the modern age. Few dispute his business savvy, his perseverance, or his technical expertise, yet critics say he is ruthless in his dealings with competitors and driven more by his desire to maintain Microsoft's dominance in the computer industry than by an interest in furthering technology.

In these books, young readers will encounter inspiring stories about real people who achieved success despite enormous obstacles. Oprah Winfrey—the most powerful, most watched, and wealthiest woman on television today—spent the first six years of her life in the care of her grandparents while her unwed mother sought work and a better life elsewhere. Her adolescence was colored by pregnancy at age fourteen, rape, and sexual abuse.

Each author documents and supports his or her work with an array of primary and secondary source quotations taken from diaries, letters, speeches, and interviews. All quotes are footnoted to show readers exactly how and where biographers derive their information and provide guidance for further research. The quotations enliven the text by giving readers eyewitness views of the life and accomplishments of each person covered in the People in the News series.

In addition, each book in the series includes photographs, annotated bibliographies, timelines, and comprehensive indexes. For both the casual reader and the student researcher, the People in the News series offers insight into the lives of today's newsmakers—people who shape the way we live, work, and play in the modern age.

From Hollywood Bad Boy to Box Office Superstar

R obert Downey Jr. is often mentioned among the best actors of his generation. Whether a role calls for serious drama, lighthearted comedy, or something in between, Downey has delivered in more than sixty films. "He consistently brings more to his material than the part demands," writes reviewer Jim Emerson. "Whether the movie itself doesn't measure up to him (*Less Than Zero, Chaplin*), or is very good indeed (*Short Cuts, Wonder Boys, Zodiac*), he contributes something that makes it— or, at least, him—something to see."[1]

Downey earned an Academy Award nomination in 1992—at the age of twenty-seven—for his masterly performance as the legendary silent film star Charlie Chaplin in *Chaplin*. Many film industry insiders predicted that it would be the first of many prestigious honors bestowed upon the exceptionally talented young actor. Within a few years, though, Downey appeared to have thrown away his once-promising career. Bored and unhappy despite his growing fame, he adopted a hard-partying lifestyle that turned him into a poster boy for Hollywood excess. Beginning in the late 1990s, Downey spiraled downward into the depths of drug addiction, was arrested multiple times, attended a variety of rehabilitation programs, and even spent time in prison. Instead of witty interviews and critical raves about

Downey's latest film project, entertainment magazines featured mug shots, court transcripts, and shocking details about his latest transgression.

From the time that Downey received his Oscar nomination, it took a full decade of failed attempts and high-profile relapses before he finally managed to make a lasting recovery from drug addiction in 2002. Even after he got clean and sober, Downey

After overcoming a downward spiral due to drug abuse in the late 1990s, Robert Downey Jr. has risen to the top of his profession.

had to work hard to restore his reputation and rebuild his acting career. He capped off his remarkable comeback in 2008 with a starring role in the blockbuster movie *Iron Man*, which became one of the highest-grossing films of all time. *New York Times Magazine* writer Chip Kidd describes Downey's career trajectory as the classic story of "a brilliant star in his field, at the top of his game, who because of hubris [pride] and bad decisions (and a large dollop of moral weakness) finds himself in dire circumstances of his own making. Just when it looks the darkest, he manages to summon his wits and willpower to overcome the demons and not only survive, but thrive. He makes himself better than he ever was."[2]

Many fans and reviewers agree that Downey's difficult journey has added even greater emotional depth to his performances. "I feel as if by some gift from a higher power, Robert Downey Jr. was sent down to Earth to help us all realize (through his work) that the human experience is a sad, funny, beautiful thing, full of imperfection and irony,"[3] says Ben Stiller, who directed Downey in his Oscar-nominated role in 2008's *Tropic Thunder*. For Downey, the experience of traveling such a hard road helped him truly appreciate his newfound peace and contentment. "I used to be so convinced that happiness was the goal, yet all those years I was chasing after it, I was unhappy in the pursuit," he explains. "Maybe the goal should really be a life that values honor, duty, good work, friends and family . . . maybe happiness follows from that."[4]

Chapter 1

Born to Be an Actor

Robert Downey Jr. was born on April 4, 1965, in Greenwich Village, a residential neighborhood on Manhattan Island in New York City. Known locally as simply "the Village," the area was home to many prominent writers and artists. His father, Robert Downey Sr., was an independent filmmaker of Russian Jewish and Irish descent. His mother, Elsie Ford Downey, was a singer and actress who came from a German and Scottish background.

Young Robert and his older sister, Allyson, were raised in what he once described as an "eccentric, far-out, and permissive"[5] home environment. His parents were hippies who actively participated in the countercultural movement of the 1960s. Their home often served as a gathering place for local actors, poets, and painters. People dropped by at all hours of the day and night to listen to music, debate current events, or collaborate on artistic works. Drugs and alcohol were an integral part of these gatherings. During his childhood, therefore, Robert witnessed both the excitement of the creative process and the lure of substance abuse.

At the time of Robert's birth, his father was just beginning to make a name for himself as a writer and director of low-budget, experimental films. His first work to receive a public screening, *Balls Bluff* (1961), was a half-hour-long, silent film about a Civil War soldier who suddenly wakes up to find himself in modern-day New York City. Downey Sr. continued making alternative films as he and his wife started a family. Elsie Downey appeared as an actress in many of the films, which tended to feature absurd ideas, surreal imagery, offbeat social commentary, or wacky comedy. Robert later explained that his mother "dedicated her life to working in accord with my dad's vision."[6]

In 1969, Downey Sr. wrote and directed a full-length feature film called *Putney Swope*. It told the story of an African American executive who mistakenly gets promoted to president of a big advertising agency. The executive creates chaos at the firm by replacing all of his white colleagues with militant black activists. Critics praised the film as a biting satire of race relations and the world of advertising, and *New York* magazine included *Putney Swope* on its list of the ten best films of the year. The film attracted a significant underground following and is considered to be a cult classic.

Film director and writer Robert Downey Sr. discusses an upcoming scene from his controversial film Putney Swope *with actress Corrine Calvert.*

Robert Downey Sr.

Robert Downey Jr. got his start as an actor by appearing in experimental films written and directed by his father, Robert Downey Sr. The elder Downey was born in Tennessee around 1937. His name at birth was Robert Elias, after his biological father. His mother, Betty McLoughlin, was a model whose image appeared on the cover of several popular magazines. After his parents split up, his mother married James Downey and moved with her son to New York City.

At the age of sixteen, young Robert left home in search of adventure. He enlisted in the U.S. Army using his stepfather's last name and a fake birth certificate, and he went by Robert Downey from that time onward. After receiving a dishonorable discharge from the service for fighting, the athletic Downey won a Golden Gloves boxing title and played semi-professional baseball for a few years.

In 1960, Downey returned to New York City, where he made a living by waiting tables, acting, writing plays and screenplays, and working for an alternative film editor. The following year, he launched his career as an independent filmmaker, which eventually encompassed nearly twenty films. Some of his early works are considered groundbreaking achievements in the underground, experimental film movement.

Robert Downey Sr. launched his career as an independent filmmaker in the underground film movement.

Launches Acting Career at Age Five

Putney Swope brought Downey Sr. a new level of success and created opportunities for him to write and direct other films. Robert made his first appearance as an actor in one of his dad's movies when he was five years old. "He did it because it was better than having a babysitter," his father explains. "But it might have led him to believe that to be creative was much better than trying to get a regular job."[7]

Young Robert's first acting role came in *Pound* (1970), a wacky social satire set in a New York City animal shelter. The movie featured eighteen human actors, each of whom portrayed a different breed of dog or cat that was waiting to be adopted. The actors dressed up in clothing that represented their breed in a humorous way. A man in a silk robe played a boxer, for example, while a man in a jogging suit played a greyhound. Robert played a puppy with an attitude.

Two years later, at the age of seven, Robert appeared in his father's first big-budget movie, *Greaser's Palace* (1972). Shot in the desert outside of Santa Fe, New Mexico, it was a surrealistic Western that loosely followed stories from the Bible. During the shooting of one scene, Robert was shocked to see an actor who was portraying God appear to kill his mother. "It could have been too much to expose him to," Downey Sr. acknowledges. "It was traumatic for him to see that kind of violence. He didn't comprehend that everybody comes back again"[8] when the scene is over.

Despite the fact that his father's movies could be strange and sometimes frightening, Robert never questioned the idea of acting in them. "From the time I was five years old, I understood acting as 'that's what we do here,'" he notes. "We do that and then we go eat pizza, or bowl, or go see a French art-film double bill."[9] Still, he understood that his family life was very unusual compared with that of his friends and classmates. "I didn't want to talk about what my dad did because it wasn't like he was directing *All in the Family* [a hit TV show of the 1970s] or anything," he says. "He was doing these crazy films. Mom would pick me up at school wearing this big quilted cape. I felt like I was in a J.D. Salinger story."[10]

Robert with his dad at an event. Downey Sr. has expressed regret about allowing young Robert to start smoking marijuana when he was eight.

Begins Using Drugs at Age Eight

Another way in which Robert's childhood was unusual was the constant presence of drugs and alcohol in his home. He once described drugs as a staple for his family. His parents and their friends frequently smoked marijuana, and occasionally did cocaine and other drugs, without bothering to hide their drug use from the children. As hippies and artists in the liberal atmosphere of the 1960s—when millions of Americans rebelled against the social constraints and conservative ideas of the past—they viewed the use of mind-altering substances as acceptable.

Robert Downey Jr. with his sister Allyson, left, and wife, Susan Downey, in 2006. When Robert's parents divorced, he stayed in New York with his mother and Allyson moved to Los Angeles with her father.

Growing up in this environment, Robert was exposed to drugs at an early age. Beginning when he was only eight years old, his father allowed him to smoke marijuana. Although Downey Sr. did not give much thought to the decision at the time, he eventually realized how irresponsible and dangerous it had been to allow the children to do drugs. "We thought it was cute to let them smoke it and all," he recalls. "It was an idiot move on our parts."[11] Robert refused to blame his father for his later drug problems, however. He claimed that his father's casual attitude toward drugs—and willingness to share them with his children—reflected the permissive nature of the times. "When my dad and I would do drugs together, it was like him trying to express his love for me in the only way he knew how,"[12] he explains.

As Robert approached his teen years, his unusual home environment took a greater toll on him emotionally and socially. Since his parents often shot their films on location, the family moved around a lot. Robert spent parts of his childhood in upstate New York, Connecticut, California, and London, England. He went to a number of different schools, and he struggled with poor grades and attendance. He tried to fit in by acting up and being the center of attention. "Our friends would dare us to streak, and he'd get buck naked and run," remembers school friend Anthony D'Eugenio. "He did it for the attention."[13]

Robert's home life got worse as he grew older. His father sank deeper into drug use, which reduced his film output and put the family into debt. His parents fought all the time, until they finally divorced in 1975. Downey Sr. moved to Los Angeles to take a job in the film industry, and Allyson decided to go along. Recognizing that his mother needed support, Robert agreed to stay with her in New York. Money was tight, however, and they could only afford a tiny, fifth-story walk-up apartment with bars on the windows. Shaken and depressed, Robert started to avoid going home. He began running around with a hard-partying group of friends and experimenting with harder drugs. "I was not dealing with my life in an effective manner," he admits. "Instead, I was creating a separate reality from the one in which I now lived and was dealing with that reality the best I could."[14]

Attends High School in California

While Robert and his mother struggled in New York, his father cleaned up his act and found some high-paying jobs in the Hollywood film industry. Every time Robert went out to visit his father, he relished the sunny, comfortable, laid-back vibe of Southern California. When he was fourteen, he decided to move across the country and make a fresh start. "I came out to California and lived with Dad," he relates. "I wanted to have, you know, a teen-age scene. You go from the one-room apartment on 48th Street to the house with the pool"[15] in Santa Monica.

After completing the eighth grade at Lincoln Junior High School in Santa Monica, Robert enrolled at Santa Monica High School. Known locally as Samohi, the school was located a few blocks from the beach. Among the student body were the sons and daughters of many big-name Hollywood talents. Robert became close friends with Ramon Estevez, the son of actor Martin Sheen and the brother of actors Charlie Sheen and Emilio Estevez.

Going to school with the offspring of famous TV and movie stars—many of whom had received formal acting, singing, and dancing lessons—made Robert feel a bit insecure about his youthful film experiences. "I didn't get trained in drama school. It was all on the job," he notes. "That [stuff] costs money; my dad was an underground filmmaker. I was faking it, to try to fit in."[16] What he lacked in formal training, however, he made up for in attitude. Robert stood out from his peers by spiking his hair, dressing in stylish punk clothes, and adopting an arrogant, outspoken manner. These qualities helped him make a place for himself among the students who focused on the performing arts. He became a member of the school's elite chorus, which won a number of singing competitions, and won a leading role in Samohi's production of the musical *Oklahoma!*

Despite his involvement in school productions, though, Robert continued to party hard after he settled in California. He often skipped school to drink alcohol with his friends. In fact, he admits that he saw no reason not to "spend every night out getting drunk [or] making a thousand phone calls in pursuit of

Santa Monica High School

Robert Downey Jr. is far from the only famous person to attend Santa Monica High School. The school, located in an affluent area just a few blocks from the Pacific Ocean, boasts a number of successful actors among its graduates. Charlie Sheen (*Wall Street, Two and a Half Men*), Emilio Estevez (*The Breakfast Club, The Mighty Ducks*), Rob Lowe (*The West Wing, Brothers & Sisters*), Sean Penn (*Mystic River, Milk*), and Dean Cain (*Lois and Clark: The New Adventures of Superman*) all attended Samohi around the same time as Downey. Other famous alumni include Robert Wagner (*Hart to Hart, Austin Powers*), Amber Tamblyn (*Joan of Arcadia, Sisterhood of the Traveling Pants*), and MTV host Carson Daly.

Samohi has also served as the setting for several movies, including the classic 1955 James Dean film *Rebel Without a Cause* and the 2009 romantic comedy *17 Again*, starring Zac Efron and Matthew Perry.

drugs."[17] As a consequence of his substance abuse, Robert got arrested for driving under the influence before he even got his driver's license. During one drinking binge, "my friend Chris Bell's mom's Mercedes suddenly became the object of my affection," he recalls. "I got my hands on the keys, I went driving, I got lost, I pulled over to ask a police officer directions before he pulled me over to ask if I had a license—and I was shortly thereafter in custody."[18]

Drops Out to Pursue Acting

Robert's alcohol and drug use took a toll on his school attendance and grades. In 1982, when he reached the end of the eleventh grade, his Samohi counselor informed him that he would have to make up work in summer school if he hoped to graduate with his class. Robert informed the counselor that he had no intention of attending summer classes and would simply drop out of high school instead. The counselor immediately called Downey Sr., hoping to enlist his support in convincing the wayward youth to stay in school. Instead, the filmmaker gave his son permission to drop out of high school, as long as he got a job and supported himself.

At the age of seventeen, Robert moved back across the country to New York City. He and his sister rented a tiny apartment near Broadway that contained only a bed, a couch, and two posters taped to the windows. He found an acting job of sorts at a nightclub called Area. Along the street, the nightclub had large glass windows in which live people pretended to be mannequins and performed the same robotic motions over and over. Robert was hired to be "the conveyor-belt operator in a space-themed installation," he recalls, "sending Gumby dolls in plastic bubbles to an undisclosed location for $10 an hour and all the brandy I could muster."[19]

Robert spent every spare moment going to auditions for acting jobs. A few months after he arrived in New York, he was cast in a play called *American Passion* by director and choreographer Pat Birch. Although it was a low-budget, Off-Off-Broadway play (one that is performed in theaters that seat fewer than 100 people), Robert approached his role with great dedication and focus. "If I didn't get there an hour and a half before curtain, I wasn't going to be ready," he relates. "The other people would roll in at a half-hour, and I'd be stretching out or doing some fake yoga, and they'd say, 'Robert's going to Nirvana before the show.' But I was the only one who got an agent two weeks later."[20] Robert Downey Jr. had officially launched the career he had been destined for since the age of five.

Chapter 2

Emerges as a Rising Star

Once he got an agent, Downey scored a number of acting roles in Hollywood movies. He started out as a supporting player in some of the popular teen-oriented movies of the 1980s. His first role came in *Baby It's You* (1983), a love story about two high school students from opposite sides of the tracks. Downey played a fellow student named Stewart. Unfortunately for him, director John Sayles ended up cutting most of his scenes out of the final version of the film. Downey can be seen in the background of one scene, but within moments he is blocked from view by an actress in the foreground. Given his fleeting appearance in the film, his friends jokingly referred to it as *Maybe It's You*.

Downey's next major film project was *Firstborn* (1984). Directed by Michael Apted, it is a drama about two suburban boys who struggle to expose their divorced mother's sinister new boyfriend. Although Downey's minor role in the film did little to advance his career, it had a major impact on his personal life. It was during the filming of *Firstborn* that Downey met Sarah Jessica Parker, who would be his girlfriend for the next seven years. The future star of *Sex and the City* was only eighteen years old at the time, but she was a professionally trained actress and dancer who had played the title role in the Broadway musical *Annie* and appeared on the family TV series *Square Pegs*. Downey and Parker fell for each other immediately and moved into an apartment together a few weeks after they

Robert Downey Jr. and Sarah Jessica Parker in a scene from Firstborn. Though it was a minor role, Robert met Sarah Jessica Parker on the set, and they immediately started a relationship.

met. Parker proved to be a steadying influence in Downey's life. "Without her, Robert would go at 100 miles an hour into a brick wall,"[21] his father declared in 1984.

Downey played a more significant role in *Weird Science* (1985), one of a string of popular teen comedies directed by John Hughes. The movie follows the antics of two nerdy young computer whizzes who use technology to create the perfect woman. Downey portrayed Ian, a bully who torments the boys but ends up losing both his girlfriend and his dignity in the end. During the filming, Downey developed a close friendship with one of his costars, Anthony Michael Hall.

Expands His Roles

Downey's relationship with Hall paid dividends in the fall of 1985. TV producer Lorne Michaels—creator of the famous late-night sketch-comedy series *Saturday Night Live*—was looking for a group of young, relatively unknown actors to fill out the cast of the show. Hall had come to his attention through his roles in *Sixteen Candles*, *The Breakfast Club*, and other teen classics of the 1980s. When Michaels invited Hall to join the cast of *Saturday Night Live*, Hall suggested that the

Downey, left, and Anthony Michael Hall, center top, developed a close friendship while working on Weird Science.

producer also give his friend Downey an audition. Downey took advantage of the opportunity and earned a spot on the show. Throughout the 1985–1986 season of *Saturday Night Live*, he amused audiences with his dead-on impersonations of famous people like singer George Michael of Wham! and actor/director Sean Penn.

While he was shooting *Saturday Night Live* in New York, Downey also made frequent trips across the country to appear in Hollywood movies. He played a fairly prominent role in *Back to School* (1986), a comedy starring Rodney Dangerfield as a jovial, self-made millionaire who decides to accompany his son to college. Downey played the son's rebellious roommate, Derek. Director Alan Metter appreciated Downey's ability to improvise and play off other actors in order to increase the comic value of certain scenes. In one scene, for example, Downey's character rushes into a room to deliver a message to Dangerfield's character. Finding a couch blocking his entrance, the actor simply vaulted over it and delivered his lines.

The charm, humor, and versatility Downey showed on *Saturday Night Live* and in his film work brought him to the attention of screenwriter/director James Toback. Toback was looking for an actor with these qualities to play the title character in his film *The Pick-Up Artist* (1987). He gave Downey the role of Jack Jericho, a smooth-talking ladies' man who falls in love with one of his conquests (played by Molly Ringwald). Downey was excited to graduate to leading-man status after playing so many supporting roles. Although *The Pick-Up Artist* received generally unfavorable reviews, it did elevate him to a new level of prominence.

Parties Hard Both On-Screen and Off

As Downey's acting career began to take off, however, his drug and alcohol use increased as well. His steadily expanding film roles gave him the resources to maintain homes in both New York and Los Angeles—both of which he shared with Parker.

His financial success also enabled him to maintain a hard-partying lifestyle as part of a crowd of hip young actors that included Billy Zane and Kiefer Sutherland. Downey and his friends drank, smoked marijuana, and soon progressed to using cocaine. Although Parker was concerned about her boyfriend's escalating substance abuse, she tried to limit its impact on his career. "I believed I was the person holding him together," she explains. "In every good and bad way I enabled him to get up in the morning and show up for work. If he did not, I was there to cover for him, find him, clean him up, and get him to the set or theatre."[22]

For his next project, Downey drew upon his own experiences to create a compelling portrait of a drug addict in the film *Less than Zero* (1987). Based on a best-selling novel by Bret Easton Ellis, the movie focuses on a group of young, attractive, and extremely wealthy—but also bored, self-absorbed, and cynical—friends hanging out and partying in Los Angeles. Downey played Julian Wells, a charismatic cocaine addict who spirals downward into debt and finally self-destructs. Although the movie received mixed reviews, critics raved about Downey's haunting performance as Julian. "In many ways, *Less than Zero* is a cynical, manipulative job," David Denby writes in *New York* magazine. "Yet, the movie has something great in it, something that could legitimately move teenagers (or anyone else): Robert Downey Jr. as the disintegrating Julian, a performance in which beautiful exuberance gives way horrifyingly to a sudden, startled sadness."[23]

Downey's performance was so convincing, however, that it made his friends and costars deeply concerned. They worried about the extent to which the decline of Julian paralleled the actor's deepening drug addiction in real life. "*Less than Zero* was a low point in his life," says Jami Gertz, who played the girlfriend that tries unsuccessfully to save Julian. "The scenes were so true to life. It was all happening to him. You had the feeling, is this guy going to make it? Is what happens to Julian going to happen to Robert?"[24] Looking back on the experience, Downey agrees that it marked a turning point in his struggle with drug addiction. "Until that movie, I took my drugs after work and on

Downney's performance as a self-destructive drug abuser in Less than Zero won him critical acclaim, but many friends worried that he was mirroring his own life in his performance.

the weekends. Maybe I'd turn up hungover on the set, but no more so than the stuntman. That changed on *Less Than Zero*," he admits. "For me, the role was like the ghost of Christmas future. The character was an exaggeration of myself. Then things changed and, in some ways, I became an exaggeration of the character."[25]

Struggles to Stay Clean

By the time Downey wrapped up filming *Less than Zero*, his substance abuse was beginning to interfere with his acting career. He gained a reputation in Hollywood as a troublemaker who had a tendency to show up late for work, appear stoned on the set, and embarrass himself in public. Downey's manager at the time, Loree Rodkin, convinced him to check himself into a month-long program at a rehabilitation center in Tucson, Arizona. Afterward, he ended up taking a year off from acting in order to get clean and sober and deal with some lingering issues from his childhood.

Upon returning to work, Downey made his first foray into big-budget action movies with *Air America* (1990). Costarring Mel Gibson, it follows the adventures of a group of American civilian pilots who fly secret missions in Southeast Asia for the U.S. Central Intelligence Agency during the Vietnam War. Downey played Billy Covington, a daring and idealistic young helicopter pilot who is recruited to join the group but grows alarmed by its illegal activities. Despite the star power of Gibson, the movie did poorly with critics and at the box office.

Downey stayed clean while shooting *Air America* in Thailand, but he started using drugs again upon his return to Los Angeles. "He's one of those tortured souls," Parker explains. She finally decided that she could not put up with it anymore and broke off their relationship. "You feel so impotent. You're always wondering and waiting for a call from someone saying, 'We went to his trailer to get him and he's dead.' I felt so sad and by the end I felt exhausted."[26]

Portrays a Screen Legend

Although he was depressed about the breakup, Downey soon found an exciting new film project to distract him from the problems in his personal life. He learned that the British director Richard Attenborough, whose biographical film *Gandhi* (1982) had won nine Academy Awards, was planning to make a movie about the life of Charlie Chaplin. Chaplin was a legendary British actor and director known as the original master of slapstick and physical comedy. During the silent film era of the 1920s, he created a loveable character called the Little Tramp, who wobbled around in a ragged, oversized suit with a bowler hat and cane. As the son of a filmmaker, Downey had idolized Chaplin from childhood and felt a spiritual connection to his work.

Like many other young actors, Downey recognized that portraying Chaplin had the potential to make him a big star. He wanted the role badly and spent a great deal of time preparing for his audition. He watched Chaplin's films, studied his movements, and worked with a dialect coach to perfect his London accent. Thanks to his intensive preparation, Downey aced his audition. He showed up at his screen test dressed in costume as the Little Tramp and performed an elaborate comedy routine in which he wrestled with a ladder. Attenborough immediately felt that Downey was perfect for the role. It helped that the director wanted to hire a lesser-known actor rather than a big star whom audiences might tend to associate with other roles.

When Attenborough announced his decision to cast Downey, however, the choice proved unpopular on many fronts. Some studio executives wanted a bigger name to play Chaplin in order to sell more tickets to the movie. Others knew about Downey's reputation as a troublemaker and worried that he might disrupt the filmmaking. Many fans of the comic legend, meanwhile, felt that only a British actor could do Chaplin justice. Downey was determined to prove the doubters wrong and make his portrayal of Chaplin a career-defining role.

Before filming began, Downey spent six months in intensive study and preparation. He worked with a coach for physical comedy to learn to move like Chaplin. He also printed out

Charlie Chaplin

Robert Downey Jr. portrayed one of his heroes, the legendary silent film star Charlie Chaplin, in the biographical movie *Chaplin* (1992). Charles Spencer Chaplin was born in London, England, on April 16, 1889. Forced to support himself from the age of ten, young Chaplin joined a juvenile theater troupe, honed his performance skills, and became a successful tap dancer and comedian on the London stage.

In 1912, Chaplin expanded his popularity to the United States with a series of vaudeville shows. He signed a motion picture contract and starred in some of the most successful films of the silent era. An innovative master of mime and slapstick comedy, he was best known for creating a disheveled yet gentlemanly character called the Little Tramp.

In 1919, Chaplin joined a group of fellow actors to found United Artists, a film production and distribution company. He won his first Academy Award for *The Circus* (1928), commented on the dehumanizing effects of industrialization in

Modern Times (1936), and warned about the rise of Adolf Hitler in *The Great Dictator* (1940). By the time his political views made him a target of Senator Joseph McCarthy's anti-Communist crusade in the 1950s, Chaplin was one of the biggest celebrities in the world. He died on December 25, 1977.

Charlie Chaplin portrays his most popular character, the "Little Tramp," in 1920.

Downey received an Oscar nomination for his portrayal of the legendary actor Charlie Chaplin in 1992.

digital photos of Chaplin's expressions and practiced them for hours in front of a mirror. Downey took lessons in order to be able to play tennis and violin left-handed, like Chaplin did. Finally, he visited a film museum in London and convinced the staff to let him try on the actual suit and boots that Chaplin wore as the Little Tramp. By the time shooting started, he was convinced that he knew more about Chaplin than anyone. "I was so crazy by the end of six and a half months of research that I told Richard Attenborough we needed to rewrite the script because there were too many things that were factually incorrect," he recalls. "They were saying, 'He's going off the deep end.'"[27]

Earns an Oscar Nomination

Downey's research paid off in an outstanding performance. Even Chaplin's daughter Geraldine, who played a role in the film, said that he captured the spirit of the man perfectly. "It was as if my father came down from heaven and inhabited and possessed him for the length of the movie,"[28] she declared. Downey's achievement was all the more remarkable because the film spanned sixty years of Chaplin's life. With the help of state-of-the-art makeup, Downey portrayed the silent film star from his late teens all the way through old age.

As a whole, *Chaplin* received mixed reviews. Some critics disliked the way Attenborough structured the film as a series of flashbacks with an elderly Chaplin looking back over his life. Others complained that the movie focused too much on Chaplin's personal life and failed to give modern audiences a sense of his impact as an actor and filmmaker. Downey's performance in the title role, however, received widespread praise. "He is good and persuasive as the adult Charlie when the material allows, and close to brilliant when he does some of Charlie's early vaudeville and film sketches," Vincent Canby writes in the *New York Times*. "His slapstick routines are graceful, witty and, most

The Academy Awards

Robert Downey Jr. officially broke into the top ranks of his profession in 1992, when he was nominated for a coveted Academy Award for Best Actor for his performance in *Chaplin*. Known informally as the Oscars, the Academy Awards are the oldest, most prestigious, and most influential form of recognition for outstanding achievement in film. The awards have been presented annually since 1929 by the nonprofit Academy of Motion Picture Arts and Sciences. Oscars are awarded in a number of categories, including Best Picture of the Year, Best Director, Best Actor/Actress in a Leading Role, and Best Actor/Actress in a Supporting Role.

The Academy Awards are handed out in February each year during a glamorous ceremony that is watched on television by hundreds of millions of people around the world. Individuals and films that are recognized typically receive a huge boost in media attention, prestige, and box office returns. Even being nominated for an Oscar is considered a tremendous honor. Downey was only twenty-seven years old when he was nominated in 1992. If he had won, he would have been the youngest Best Actor recipient in the history of the Academy Awards. Downey earned a second nomination, in the Best Supporting Actor category, in 2009 for *Tropic Thunder*.

important, really funny."[29] Online reviewer Jeffrey M. Anderson adds that "Downey not only imitates Chaplin, but also captures his essence, and the complex joy and sadness that must have come from being the most famous man in the world. He makes you laugh with his effortless slapstick and makes you cry with his heartbreak."[30]

Downey received a number of prestigious awards for his work, including a Golden Globe as Best Actor in a Drama and Best Actor honors from the British Academy of Film and Television Arts. He was nominated for an Academy Award for Best

Actor—and many film industry insiders felt that he deserved to win—but instead the Oscar went to Al Pacino for his role in *Scent of a Woman* (1992). Still, Downey was thrilled to receive such recognition before he even reached the age of thirty. "I felt like I had just knocked one out of the park," he notes. "I thought, 'You know what? This is the big turning point for me.'"[31]

Though he did not get the Oscar for Best Actor, Downey did take home a Golden Globe Best Actor award for Chaplin.

After pouring such intensive energy and focus into *Chaplin*, however, Downey experienced an emotional letdown. He tried to mask these feelings by resuming his hard-partying lifestyle. "There was this kind of lull, and I never really found any momentum to focus my creative energy after that, so pretty much expectable things happened,"[32] he explains. "You'd have thought that at some point I'd sit down and say, 'OK, I just got nominated for *Chaplin;* what I do in the next eighteen months is really key, so maybe I should cut my bong intake in half and focus on what my plan is.'"[33] Instead, after Downey came so close to reaching the pinnacle of success for an actor, his life and career began spiraling downward.

Chapter 3

Caught in a Downward Spiral

All the professional recognition that Downey received for his performance in *Chaplin* did little to help him resolve his personal issues. He continued to struggle with depression over the end of his relationship with Sarah Jessica Parker. In addition, the emotional letdown he experienced following his Oscar nomination made it difficult for him to decide upon a suitable follow-up project. As before, Downey often dealt with his feelings in a reckless and self-destructive way—by drinking and doing drugs.

While partying at a friend's house in the spring of 1992, Downey met Deborah Falconer. She worked as a model and nightclub hostess, but she aspired to become a singer and songwriter. Although the couple hit it off immediately, their relationship had a bit of a rough start. A group of Downey's family and friends interrupted their first date by staging an intervention. The group confronted him about his substance abuse and encouraged him to seek treatment. "They were all looking at me like I was the devil's child,"[34] Falconer remembers. As a casual drug user herself at that time, Falconer ignored the warnings about Downey's addiction. The couple got married on May 29, 1992—only six weeks after they had met.

Shortly after the wedding, Downey and his new bride moved into a modern home north of Malibu, California. Its most appealing feature was the large bank of picture windows overlooking the Pacific Coast. Falconer became pregnant within a few

Robert Downey married Deborah Falconer on May 29, 1992, just six weeks after they had met.

months, and their son, Indio, was born on September 7, 1993. Downey asked his good friend Anthony Michael Hall to serve as the boy's godfather. Although Downey loved being a father and doted on his son, marriage and parenthood were not enough to make him settle down and abandon his partying ways.

Treading Water

In his search for a challenging follow-up to *Chaplin*, Downey appeared in three very different movies over the next year. The most revealing was a feature-length documentary film called *The Last Party* (1993), which chronicled the 1992 presidential race between Democrat Bill Clinton and Republican George H.W. Bush. Although Downey did not have a strong background in politics, he agreed to serve as its on-screen narrator. He criss-crossed the country with a film crew in tow—attending parades, marches, rallies, and both parties' national conventions—to talk with people about various political issues. Over the course of the movie, however, Downey also talks very candidly about his personal life, including his unusual family background and his parents' divorce. *New York Times* reviewer Stephen Holden claims that *The Last Party* creates a portrait of "America as a dys-functional family," adding that this image "plays neatly into Mr. Downey's own personal drama."[35]

Downey also took advantage of an opportunity to work with Robert Altman, an award-winning director known for his exper-imental, improvisational filmmaking style. He accepted a small role in Altman's ensemble film *Short Cuts* (1993), which was adapted from a series of interconnected short stories by Ray-mond Carver. Downey played Bill, a Hollywood makeup artist, and shared screen time with a large cast of well-known actors. The film received positive reviews, with *Variety* describing it as a "complex and full-bodied human comedy."[36]

Downey's biggest acting challenge came in his role as the self-absorbed business executive Thomas Reilly in the romantic comedy *Heart and Souls* (1993). The story begins with Thomas's birth in a car that is involved in an accident on its way to the hospital. The accident claims the lives of four strangers (played by Charles Grodin, Kyra Sedgwick, Tom Sizemore, and Alfre Woodard), who end up watching over Thomas as guardian an-gels throughout his life. When Thomas is thirty, the four souls learn that they must use him to achieve their unfulfilled dreams in order to reach heaven. From this point on, the souls take turns inhabiting Thomas's body, with hilarious results. Downey

Short Cuts cast members, left to right, Lili Taylor, Robert Downey Jr., Christopher Penn, and Jennifer Jason Leigh on the movie set. Downey received critical acclaim for his work in the Robert Altman film.

not only plays his own character, he also performs impersonations of the other four actors when their characters take over Thomas's body. Janet Maslin of the *New York Times* calls him "an amazing mimic. The best thing about the film is the chance to watch his uncanny impersonations of his co-stars."[37]

Drugs Take a Toll

For a while, Downey's substance abuse did not have much impact on his work. Since alcohol and drug use was relatively common in Hollywood, many people had a tendency to overlook his excesses. By the mid-1990s, however, his addiction began to take a bigger toll on both his career and his personal life. This change occurred when Downey moved beyond marijuana and cocaine and began smoking black-tar heroin. Produced in Mexico, this form of heroin is very pure and addictive. It is also widely available and relatively cheap in the western United States.

Shortly after he began using heroin, Downey appeared in *Home for the Holidays* (1995), a film about a dysfunctional family that gathers for Thanksgiving with funny and heart-wrenching results. He played Tommy Larson, the family's mischievous gay brother. Although Downey turned in a good performance, he later admitted that he had been high on heroin throughout the filming. His behavior—and his casual attitude about it—bothered director Jodie Foster so much that she wrote him a letter begging him to get help. Downey recalls that the letter said: "I know what's going on and I think you know that I know what's going on. I'm not worried about you on this film because it's kind of,

In the 1993 movie **Heart and Souls** *Downey Jr (center) starred with and did screen impersonations of the characters played by (left to right) Tom Sizemore, Charles Grodin, Kyra Sedgwick, and Alfre Woodard.*

Heroin Addiction

Heroin is a potent narcotic drug derived from the seed pods of opium poppy plants. Classified by the U.S. government as an illegal, controlled substance, it is synthesized from the prescription painkiller morphine. Recreational drug users typically inject, smoke, or snort heroin to get high. Heroin acts on the brain very quickly to produce an intense feeling of euphoria or relaxation. Large doses of heroin are toxic and can be fatal.

Tolerance for heroin develops rapidly, and frequent use carries a high risk of physical and psychological dependence or addiction. People who become addicted to heroin often suffer painful physical symptoms upon discontinuing use. Common withdrawal symptoms include aches and pains, cramps, tremors, chills, sweating, nausea, depression, and anxiety. The severe side effects of withdrawal, which can last for up to a week, make it extremely difficult for addicts to break their dependency on heroin.

Heroin is derived from the opium poppy and is a highly addictive narcotic.

like, safe. . . . I'm worried about what will happen if you think you can do this again."[38] Convinced that he had the situation under control, Downey ignored Foster's advice.

The problem became more difficult to overlook with Downey's next project, a period drama called *Restoration* (1995). He starred as Robert Merviel, a young doctor whose service to the court of King Charles II results in a series of misadventures. Although critics praised the quirky charm of Downey's performance in the film, they could not help but notice his odd and erratic behavior during promotional appearances. He often showed up late or abruptly canceled scheduled interviews, for instance. He also insisted upon flying a "friend," who turned out to be a drug dealer, to meet him in Germany.

As time passed, Downey's heroin addiction affected his work in increasingly obvious ways. He often partied all night and then showed up late on the set or fell asleep between takes. The drug use also affected Downey's appearance. He lost weight and began to look thin, pale, and shaky on camera. The change was shockingly apparent in the film *Hugo Pool* (1997), directed by his father, in which Downey played an eccentric Dutch filmmaker named Franz Mazur. Although the role called for him to behave strangely, Downey admits that his bizarre, over-the-top performance was drug induced. "I was just in a bad place," he states. "But it's a cult favorite among some of my peers because I was, like, 138 pounds and it was beyond improvisation. It's like, 'Wow, he's literally bouncing this performance off some space shuttle far away!'"[39] Critics noticed that something was wrong with Downey. *Los Angeles Times* reviewer Jack Mathews called it "one of the worst performances he or any major star has recorded on film. . . . Given the actor's off-camera adventures, it's hard not to regard it as the work of someone who's not thinking straight."[40]

At one point, some of Downey's friends grew so concerned about him that they decided to force him into drug treatment. Actor/director Sean Penn showed up at his house with a couple of other friends, broke down his door, wrestled him out of bed, and hustled him into a waiting car. They drove him to the airport, where a private plane was waiting to transport him to the live-in rehabilitation center he had visited once before in Tucson, Arizona. Downey only remained at the center for three days before he made his escape, however. He hitchhiked to the nearest airport and called his accountant to arrange a flight back to Los Angeles.

Arrested Three Times in One Month

Downey's substance abuse also started to cause problems at home during this time. His wife had stopped using drugs when she became pregnant. Once their son was born, she tried to convince Downey to get clean in order to set a good example for him. Fatherhood did not provide the push Downey needed to beat his addiction, however. In April 1996, Falconer finally gave up trying to change her husband. She moved out and took Indio with her. "I have a sadness that we separated, but the process of evolution is always changing. We separated, but we're still connected," she explains. "Our greatest accomplishment is Indio— that speaks for itself. There's so much love that has come from that."[41]

The breakup of his family sent Downey into a downward spiral. He lost control and ended up being arrested three times within a month. The first incident occurred on June 23, 1996, when Downey was pulled over for speeding and driving erratically on the Pacific Coast Highway near Malibu. The police report said that he appeared confused and acted strangely, which convinced the patrolman that he was under the influence of a controlled substance. A search of Downey's vehicle turned up cocaine, heroin, and a .357 Magnum handgun. Downey was arrested and taken to jail, but he posted bail of ten thousand dollars and was released later that night. His mug shots and stories about his arrest appeared on television news programs and the cover of tabloid magazines across the country.

On July 16—only ten days before his scheduled court appearance for the first incident—Downey got in trouble with the law again. Under the influence of drugs and alcohol, the actor tried to return to his home in Malibu. Instead, he mistakenly entered the home of a neighboring family with three young children.

Not realizing his error, Downey stumbled into an eight-year-old boy's room, stripped down to his underwear, and passed out on the bed. The boy's mother, Lisa Curtis, found him a short time later and called the police to report a stranger in her house. "He seems to have passed out in my child's bed," Curtis told the 911 operator. "We kind of shook him and he would moan and kind of talk but he seems to just go right back to sleep."[42] Downey was arrested and charged with being under the influence of a controlled substance and trespassing.

A handcuffed Robert Downey Jr. arrives at a Malibu, California, courthouse on July 22, 1996, to plead not guilty to drug and weapons charges.

Treatment for Heroin Addiction

Heroin addiction is a chronic, relapsing disease that involves both physical and psychological components. A variety of treatments are available to help people recover from heroin addiction. The effectiveness of different treatment options depends on the individual. Most treatments address the addict's physical dependence on the drug, which causes painful withdrawal symptoms upon discontinuing use, as well as various behavioral or environmental factors that contribute to the addict's substance abuse.

Detoxification programs work to eliminate heroin from an addict's system while helping to manage withdrawal symptoms. One method of detoxification that has proved effective for many addicts is methadone. Methadone is a synthetic opiate drug that blocks the effects of heroin and eliminates withdrawal symptoms in heroin users. The main downside to methadone is that, like heroin, it carries a risk of dependence.

Detoxification programs are usually followed by psychological or behavioral treatments, which can be administered on an outpatient or residential basis. These treatments are intended to help recovering addicts modify their behavior, gain new skills to cope with stressful situations, and develop a lasting commitment to healthy living.

Although the second charge was later dropped, the shocking "Goldilocks incident" put Downey back in the headlines. Many reporters described it as a tragedy that such a brilliant actor had fallen victim to the devastating effects of addiction. "I don't know what the demon is that really drives Robert," said his manager Loree Rodkin. "If any of us knew, we could save him. I really thought that the first time he got [in trouble], it would have been a wake-up call. But he's never been this self-destructive.

Every day I keep my fingers crossed that I'm not going to read that he's dead."[43]

When Downey answered the new charges on July 18, the judge ordered him to receive inpatient treatment at the Exodus Recovery Center in Marina del Rey, California. Two days later, however, he climbed through a bathroom window at the center and took a taxi to a friend's house, where he proceeded to get high. When the police caught up with him, Downey was arrested yet again for leaving the rehab center in violation of the court order. This time, he remained in jail for several weeks while he awaited further court appearances. Toward the end of July, a thin, haggard, remorseful Downey stood before Judge Lawrence Mira wearing a prison jumpsuit and handcuffs. As his parents and his estranged wife looked on, he told the judge that he recognized the seriousness of his drug addiction and was determined to beat it. Mira responded by sentencing him to several months at a full-time, supervised drug rehabilitation facility, followed by three years' probation and frequent, random drug tests. Downey's many fans hoped that the sentence would enable him to get clean and turn his life around before it was too late.

Chapter 4

Travels a Rough Road to Recovery

Movie fans and celebrity watchers followed the dramatic story of Downey's descent into drug addiction with a mix of horror and fascination. His three arrests within a month received extensive coverage on TV news and in entertainment magazines during the summer of 1996. The reports generally presented Downey as a Hollywood bad boy who had spun out of control and squandered his considerable talent. Although Downey would have preferred to keep his struggles with addiction private, he understood the strong public interest in his story. "I'm as easily drawn into the gossip cesspool as anyone else," he admits. "Definitely, on certain days, reading about someone's demise is infinitely more attractive to me than reading about somebody having a breakthrough, or an epiphany."[44]

Partly due to all the publicity surrounding his legal problems, Downey remained a hot commodity in the entertainment business. He received a number of job offers during the months he spent in court-ordered drug rehabilitation. In November 1996, for example, he was allowed to leave the rehab facility for a weekend and travel to New York in order to serve as the host of *Saturday Night Live*. He confronted his recent string of misdeeds in a humorous way during his opening monologue. After telling the audience that he brought slides from his summer vacation, Downey proceeded to show images of himself sleeping in a crib, accepting a suspicious package, and sitting in a jail cell. By poking fun at his problems, Downey seemed to indicate that he would be able to overcome them.

Shortly after Downey was released from the rehab facility in 1997, he starred in a film written and directed by his friend James Toback. *Two Girls and a Guy* (1997) tells the story of Blake Allen, a charismatic but self-absorbed actor who is dating two women at the same time. When both of the women show up at his upscale New York City apartment unexpectedly, Allen must face up to his deception. In a review for the *New York Times*, Janet Maslin argues that Downey's charming performance saved the movie. "Played less winningly, [Allen] could infuriate women and turn men green with envy," she writes. "Played by Mr. Downey, he's a bristling, clever, volatile one-man show."[45]

After his release from rehabilitation, Downey worked with friend and director James Toback in **Two Girls and a Guy.**

Suffers a Relapse

Downey won roles in other high-profile films following his release from rehab. He played a private investigator in *The Gingerbread Man* (1998), based on a John Grisham novel, and he played an FBI agent in *U.S. Marshals* (1998), the sequel to the hugely successful 1993 action film *The Fugitive*. Keeping busy with work did not keep him out of trouble for long, however. In September 1997 he suffered a relapse and started drinking and taking drugs again. Before long, he failed a court-ordered drug test. In December he found himself back in court for violating the terms of his probation.

Standing before Judge Lawrence Mira, Downey apologized for his actions and asked for more time to conquer his addiction. "I've been addicted to drugs in one form or another since I

When Downey appeared before Judge Lawrence Mira for violating his probation Mira sentenced Downey to prison, saying, "I'm going to send you to jail. . . . I don't care who you are."

was eight years old,"[46] he explained. His pleas failed to sway the judge. Hoping that a tough stance would scare Downey straight, Mira sentenced him to spend 111 days in prison at the Twin Towers Correctional Facility in Los Angeles. "You need to find out why . . . you are willing to endure so much pain and turmoil in your life to continue doing drugs," Mira declared. "I'm going to send you to jail. . . . I don't care who you are."[47]

For the next four months, Downey lived much like the other six thousand prisoners at Twin Towers. He spent most of his time reading in his cell. He was allowed to watch TV for an hour per day and take a shower twice per week. Although he was permitted to have visitors, Downey refused to see anyone. "I think he's embarrassed," said his longtime friend and business partner Joe Bilella. "I don't think I would want a lot of people visiting me in jail either. What's he gonna say? 'Hey, how's it going? Here's all my new friends?' There's nothing great about it."[48]

On February 13, 1998, Downey got into a fight with a fellow inmate. He ended up with a cut on his face that required six stitches. Since his physical appearance is so important to his work, prison authorities released the actor briefly so that he could have the wound treated by a plastic surgeon. Downey's actual release from prison came on March 31, 1998. He went directly to a live-in rehabilitation center, where he remained until August 7. When Downey finally emerged, having completed his sentence, many people close to him hoped that the experience would help him turn his life around. "All you can say with someone who has an addiction is, you hope for the best," said his attorney Ira Reiner. "I can't say, and no one can, that Robert will succeed. But I can say, based on the dozens of conversations I've had with him, that he really does want to stay sober."[49]

Spends a Year in Prison

The hopes for Downey's recovery seemed promising at first. He succeeded in his personal battle against drug addiction for about nine months. During this period of sobriety, he shot the

During a nine-month period of sobriety, Downey worked with Michael Douglas in the critically acclaimed film Wonder Boys.

critically acclaimed movie *Wonder Boys* (2000). Downey played Terry Crabtree, a book editor who makes a visit to a college town to encourage a frustrated English professor to finish his long-awaited novel. As usual, Downey received positive reviews for his performance. Offscreen, however, he continued to experience problems in his personal life. Legal bills depleted his savings, and the Internal Revenue Service placed a lien on his house for unpaid taxes. Downey ended up sleeping on the couch at various friends' houses.

In the face of mounting pressures, Downey started using drugs again in the spring of 1999. "I found myself not having my priorities straight and I relapsed,"[50] he noted. He skipped court-ordered drug tests in violation of his probation, and he was forced to undergo a psychiatric evaluation. When he appeared before Mira in August, Downey admitted that his addiction was out of control. "It's like I've got a shotgun in my mouth, and my finger's on the trigger, and I like the taste of gunmetal,"[51] he stated. The judge responded by issuing an even harsher sentence than before. Mira revoked Downey's three-year probation and sentenced him to spend that amount of time—less 201 days he had already served—at the California Substance Abuse Treatment Facility and State Prison in Corcoran.

Downey's many supporters were outraged by the sentence. They argued that nonviolent drug offenders should receive treatment for their addiction rather than incarceration. Some of his fans even started an online petition calling for his release. Downey, on the other hand, felt that the sentence was appropriate. "I think that for people like me who have all the opportunities in the world to have a great life but instead choose to destroy themselves, jail is definitely an answer," he says. "It's not pleasant, it's not fun. In my case, though, it was probably necessary."[52]

Downey spent one year at the California Substance Abuse Treatment Center and was released in August 2000.

Celebrities in Prison

Robert Downey Jr. is just one name on a long list of celebrities whose struggles with substance abuse have landed them in prison. Some of the other famous people who have spent time behind bars include Kelsey Grammer (*Frasier*), Kiefer Sutherland (*24*), Michelle Rodriguez (*Lost*), Paris Hilton (*The Simple Life*), and Lindsay Lohan (*Freaky Friday, Mean Girls*). Some mental health experts worry that the parade of celebrities going to jail—and the media frenzy that accompanies their incarceration—may have a negative impact on young fans. They argue that the publicity surrounding famous inmates serves to glorify the prison experience and desensitize young people to the negative consequences of substance abuse.

Downey spent the next year sharing a medium-security cell with four other inmates. He worked in the kitchen at the facility for wages of eight cents an hour and sang in the prison chorus. He also took the General Educational Development exam to earn his high school equivalency diploma. This time, Downey accepted visitors, viewing it as an opportunity to reconnect with his family and friends. Although he tried to make the best of the situation, he recognized that being in prison forced him to miss out on many things. "Watching the Oscars from jail was a trip, a real trip," he acknowledges. "But, you know, people are people. I wasn't thinking about my own tragic situation. I was going, 'I didn't expect her to win. Isn't that nice?' I was just another schmuck watching it, you know?"[53]

In August 2000 Downey was released from prison. His freedom came earlier than expected because his lawyers convinced the court to give him additional credit for the time he had already served. Still, spending a year behind bars made an impact on Downey. Describing the experience as "awful" and "horrible,"[54] he left prison determined to straighten himself out and avoid going back. He checked himself into Walden House, a residential drug treatment facility in Los Angeles, to continue the hard work of recovery. "Addiction is addiction and I'm an addict who has to fight for the rest of his life against the allure of substance abuse," he explains. "Every day that I'm clean is a step in the right direction. But every day poses a risk that I can fall back and Hollywood is a palace of temptation. So I'm waging my fight against that backdrop, but I feel good about my life right now."[55]

Launches a Comeback on TV

Despite taking a year off from acting, Downey still had many friends in Hollywood who were eager to see him back at work. Even though everyone respected his talent, many people were reluctant to take the risk of hiring him. If he suffered another relapse and returned to prison, it could cause a costly disruption in production or even force the cancellation of a film project. The companies that provided insurance to the major film studios refused to cover Downey for this reason. Luckily for him, a few people believed in him enough to give him a chance. One of these supporters was David E. Kelley, the writer and producer of hit TV series like *L.A. Law*, *Chicago Hope*, *Picket Fences*, and *The Practice*.

Kelley offered Downey a role on his successful legal comedy/drama *Ally McBeal*. Downey played an attorney, Larry Paul, who emerges as an important new love interest for the main character (played by Calista Flockhart). He brought his considerable energy and charm to the role and developed great on-screen chemistry with Flockhart. In fact, many reviewers credited his addition to the cast with revitalizing the show, which was widely held to have lost its creative focus. Downey's impressive comeback received extensive coverage in the press, and many fans dared to hope that the actor had beaten his addiction once and for all.

Unfortunately, Downey's recovery faltered once again in November 2000. His estranged wife, Deborah Falconer, officially filed for divorce after more than four years of separation. When

Downey took home the Golden Globe and Screen Actors'
Guild awards for his work in Ally McBeal. But he was
arrested again and fired from the show.

he got the papers, Downey became depressed and turned to
drugs. "It was my lowest point in terms of addictions," he acknowledges. "At that stage, I didn't give a [whit] whether I ever
acted again."[56] He was arrested at a Palm Springs resort over
Thanksgiving for possession of cocaine and valium, though he
remained free on bail while the case wound its way through the
courts.

In January 2001 the Hollywood Foreign Press Association
recognized Downey's performance in *Ally McBeal* with a Golden
Globe Award for Best Supporting Actor in a TV series. A few
months after he accepted the award, though, Downey got arrested again. A police officer saw him trying to buy drugs in an

alley on the west side of Los Angeles on April 24, 2001, and determined that he was under the influence of a controlled substance. It turned out to be the last straw for Kelley. He fired Downey and wrote his character out of *Ally McBeal*. "We are wrapping up the stories for the final few episodes for the season without him," said a statement released by Kelley's production company. "Robert is a unique talent and a very special person, and we wish him the best and hope for his full recovery."[57]

By the time Downey's two latest cases made it to trial, however, the legal environment had changed. The Substance Abuse

Insurance in the Film Industry

As Robert Downey Jr. struggled to overcome drug addiction and legal problems, he found it difficult to land acting jobs. Part of the problem was that he was unable to get insurance.

Producing a movie or television show is time-consuming and expensive. There is always a risk that some unforeseen problem could crop up to interrupt, postpone, or even cancel a project while it is in production. The director could become ill, for instance, or a storm could destroy a set or damage equipment.

Before any film project gets approved, therefore, production companies take out insurance policies to protect their investment and compensate them for financial losses. These insurance policies cover cast members, camera operators, producers, and other key people whose injury, illness, or death would disrupt filming. Insurance companies often require these individuals to undergo medical examinations or submit health histories before they provide coverage. If an actor has a history of substance abuse, insurance companies consider them to pose a high risk and often deny coverage.

and Crime Prevention Act, also known as Proposition 36, had been passed by California voters and was scheduled to take effect on July 1, 2001. The new law required nonviolent drug offenders to receive treatment in a rehabilitation facility rather than be sentenced to prison until at least their third offense. Respecting the intent of voters, Judge Randall White was relatively lenient. He sentenced Downey to spend one year at a residential drug rehab facility called Wavelengths, followed by three years' probation and random drug testing. The judge warned, however, that the actor would face up to four years in prison if he was arrested again. While acknowledging his past mistakes, Downey expressed determination to move forward. "It's like the boy who cried wolf," he said. "I'm not going to say what I'm going to do. It's not going to be damage control. You know, there's nothing worse than a reformed anything. I just want my [expletive deleted] life back."[58]

Chapter 5

Makes a Cautious Comeback

After completing his court-ordered year at the Wavelengths drug rehabilitation center in the summer of 2002, Downey finally managed to remain clean and sober. He cites July 4, 2002, as the date when his recovery from drug addiction truly took hold. "The country's independence, my independence,"[59] he notes.

During rehab, Downey spent countless hours thinking deeply about his personal background and formative experiences. He emerged with a clearer perspective on his life. "I invested a lot of time in rebellion, self-destruction, and random acts of insanity," he explains. "I think I grew up feeling like a lot of LA kids—I didn't know what to do with myself except that I knew I wasn't happy with what life was offering around me. I was restless, I didn't have as much attention from my father as I think I needed, and I became a typical wild Hollywood teenager. And I continued that reckless behavior into my adult life."[60]

As part of his recovery process, Downey found new, positive outlets for his energy and rebellious nature. He discovered martial arts, especially an ancient form of kung fu called Wing Chun. Downey practiced with an accomplished teacher, Eric Oram, who taught him to combine power and aggression with relaxation and structure. Wing Chun not only kept him in shape physically, but it also helped him maintain mental discipline and spiritual calm. Downey felt so strongly about Wing Chun that he promoted it on the daytime talk show *The Oprah*

Downey gives the press a thumbs up as he leaves a court hearing in 2002 to report on his rehabilitation efforts.

Winfrey Show, telling host Oprah Winfrey that it gave him "a sense of spiritual warriordom."[61]

In addition to Wing Chun, Downey also took up yoga and meditation to help him avoid temptation and achieve emotional balance. He switched to a diet of natural and whole foods, and he traveled with a massage therapist and an herbalist, both of whom also contributed to his well-being. "Once you have that support," Downey says, "why would you fare as well without it? It's like, you know, if you become a more effective engine, you need more maintenance."[62]

Breaks Back In to Acting

Once he rounded up the needed support, Downey felt confident that he had turned the corner in his recovery from drug addiction. He found it difficult to convince people in Hollywood that he would be able to stay clean this time, however. "The hard

Wing Chun

Robert Downey Jr. gives some of the credit for his recovery from drug addiction to his discovery of Wing Chun kung fu. Wing Chun is a Chinese martial art that teaches practitioners techniques of self-defense and close combat.

According to legend, Wing Chun originated in the seventeenth century when a Manchurian minority took control of China and oppressed the Han majority. Han men were forbidden from practicing martial arts or owning weapons. Five Han grand masters met secretly in a Buddhist temple to combine the most effective techniques from a variety of ancient martial arts into one discipline. Although the Manchurians destroyed the temple, knowledge of the discipline survived in the form of a Buddhist nun, Ng Mui, who passed it down to a young woman named Yim Wing Chun.

The discipline of Wing Chun emphasizes biomechanics—body structure, positioning, and balance—rather than brute strength. Practitioners are supposed to be firm but flexible, like bamboo. In addition to physical conditioning, the martial art gives practitioners a sense of well-being and spiritual calm. "I can't even describe how much Wing Chun has impacted my ability to stay well and focused," Downey states. "It has changed my life."

Quoted in Los Angeles Wing Chun Kung Fu Academy. www.lawingchun.com.

thing is going to be convincing people who are putting up huge sums of money that there's not going to be any problems,"[63] confirmed producer Mark Burg, who had worked with Downey on *The Gingerbread Man*. All of the major film studios purchase insurance policies to protect their investment in case something happens to one of the actors before or during the shooting of a movie. Downey had spent so much time in rehab and prison, though, that the insurance companies refused to cover him.

Downey found himself in a tough situation. He could not work as an actor without insurance, and he could not get insurance without proving that he was a reliable actor. He needed help to break back in to the acting business. It came from his friend Mel Gibson, who had worked with Downey on *Air America* and had experienced his own problems with alcoholism. Gibson offered Downey the starring role in a new film he was producing called *The Singing Detective* (2003). He also agreed to pay for Downey's insurance policy out of his own pocket.

Friend Mel Gibson put up the insurance money for Downey in 2003 so he could work on **The Singing Detective**. *The film was a box office flop but Downey received acclaim for his performance.*

Based on a popular British TV series, *The Singing Detective* told the story of Dan Dark, a writer of detective novels who suffers from a painful and debilitating skin condition. Stuck in a hospital bed, Dark imagines an elaborate fantasy life in which he sings, dances, and solves mysteries. The role required Downey to act beneath grotesque, rubbery makeup in the hospital scenes, as well as to showcase his musical talents in the fantasy sequences. "I don't know who else could have done it," says director Keith Gordon. "From the darkest depths to the silly comedy to the singing and dancing, Robert has that ability to change gears emotionally."[64] Although *The Singing Detective* was a flop at the box office, it provided critics with a vivid reminder of Downey's wide-ranging abilities. With Gibson vouching for him, it also gave the actor a valuable foothold to climb back into the film industry.

Finds Love and Stability

A string of new projects followed quickly for the actor, including a role in the thriller *Gothika* (2003). Downey played a psychiatrist who treats a woman who is accused of murdering her husband but has no memory of committing the crime. Although the film was poorly received by critics, making it turned out to have a tremendous impact on Downey's life. One of *Gothika*'s producers was a bright, attractive young woman named Susan Levin. Downey was interested in her right away, but she thought he was strange and rejected his advances. He persisted, though, and Levin finally agreed to go out with him after they finished shooting the movie.

After Downey and Levin had dated for about six months, he proposed marriage on November 6, 2003—her thirtieth birthday. She accepted with the stipulation that he must remain clean and sober. "She's been very firm that if he's going to be with her, he has to really toe the line,"[65] says Joel Silver, one of Levin's coproducers. Downey eagerly agreed to the terms. His divorce from Deborah Falconer was finalized in the spring of 2004, and he exchanged vows with Levin on August 27, 2005, at the Windy Dunes estate in upstate New York. The couple

In 2003's Gothika Downey played a psychiatrist treating a woman, played by Halle Berry, who cannot remember murdering her husband.

honeymooned in the south of France. Downey claims that his second marriage gave him a sense of happiness, fulfillment, and contentment that helped him move beyond his earlier problems. "I'm not the poster boy for anything anymore," he states. "I don't . . . relate to that time in my life. Because it is something that I transcended, somehow, with really a lot of . . . love and support."[66]

With Levin's encouragement, Downey found a new outlet for his creative energies. He recorded an album of music. "My vice, it seems now, is creativity," he declares. "It's all about living a normal, balanced life."[67] Downey had taught himself to play the piano as a boy, and he always took a keyboard with him on film locations to help him relax and unwind. Over the years, he had composed a number of songs about his experiences and interests. Downey first came to public attention as a singer and musician during his stint on *Ally McBeal*. His character, Larry Paul, often played the piano at his apartment and sometimes sang at the bar where the employees from Ally's law firm hung out after hours. Downey's musical interludes were so popular with fans of the show that he ended up performing several songs on the *Ally McBeal* soundtrack album.

Downey's own album, *The Futurist* (2004), consists of eight original songs plus a couple of covers, including Charlie Chaplin's famous ballad "Smile." All of the tracks showcase Downey's smoky voice—which critics often compare with Peter Gabriel's or Bob Seger's—against spare, jazzy arrangements featuring him on the piano. Although the album received mediocre reviews, Downey's many fans snapped up copies anyway. Downey is proud of *The Futurist*, even though he recognizes that his fame as a troubled actor created the opportunity for him to record it. "No way would I ever get to express myself musically if I wasn't an actor of ill repute," he acknowledges. "You don't get on 'Oprah' if you live a gleaming life and then just happen to cross over into music."[68]

Overcomes His Bad Reputation

As more time passed without Downey suffering a relapse, he slowly managed to rebuild his reputation. He churned out solid performances in ten films between 2005 and 2007. For example, Downey played reporter Joe Wershba in *Good Night, and Good Luck* (2005), the critically acclaimed biography of legendary journalist Edward R. Murrow. He also ventured into family comedy, portraying the sinister animal researcher Dr. Kozak in Disney's *The Shaggy Dog* (2006). In 2007, Downey played a hard-drinking journalist on the trail of a serial killer in *Zodiac*, as well as a high school principal who matches wits with a cocky new student in *Charlie Bartlett*. Although most of his

Susan Levin Downey

Robert Downey Jr. found happiness and contentment with his second wife, Susan. Susan Levin was born in Chicago on November 6, 1973. She was determined to make a career in the film industry from the age of twelve. After graduating as valedictorian from Schaumburg High School in Illinois, she earned a bachelor's degree from the University of Southern California's School of Cinema and Television.

In 1995, Levin took a job with New Line Cinema, where she did uncredited production work on the Mortal Kombat series of martial arts movies. In 1999, she moved to Silver Pictures, a production company owned by Joel Silver. She proved to be a smart and ambitious employee and quickly increased her responsibilities. In 2002, Levin received her first full-credit producer job on the thriller *Gothika*, where she met and began dating her future husband.

Levin married Robert Downey Jr. on August 27, 2005. The spouses enjoyed working together on such films as *Kiss Kiss Bang Bang, Sherlock Holmes,* and *Iron Man 2*. In 2009, Susan Downey left Silver Pictures to launch a new production company, Team Downey, to develop film projects in conjunction with her husband.

Robert Downey Jr. wed Susan Levin on August 27, 2005.

films received decent reviews and performed respectably at the box office, none of them became a huge hit.

Downey had especially high hopes for *Kiss Kiss Bang Bang* (2005), which Benjamin Svetkey of *Entertainment Weekly* calls a "savvy, twisty 2005 crime caper."[69] Downey played Harry Lockhart, a small-time New York thief who stumbles into an acting audition while running from the police. He ends up landing the part by giving a moving speech about the perils of a life of crime. The filmmakers send Lockhart to Hollywood, where he teams up with a Los Angeles police officer (played by Val Kilmer) to research his role as a thief. Critics praised *Kiss Kiss Bang Bang* for its combination of stylized action and dark humor, but—to Downey's great disappointment—it did not last long in movie theaters. "It was going to be my coming-out party, my emergence into 21st-century cinema," he says. "When it tanked, I was heartbroken."[70]

Kiss Kiss Bang Bang was still notable, though, because it featured the acting debut of Downey's son, Indio, as a younger version of Lockhart. Indio enjoyed working with his dad, but he quickly abandoned acting in favor of music. Indio had shown talent from an early age as a songwriter and guitar player. He and some teenage friends formed a band called the Jack Bambis. With the support of some celebrity fans, the band played some high-profile gigs and even served as the opening act at a Pearl Jam concert.

A major benefit of Downey's new, stable lifestyle was that it gave him the opportunity to spend more time with his son. Indio often came to visit him and Susan at their rented house in Brentwood, on the west side of Los Angeles. Downey appreciated how far he had come to achieve a normal family life. "I feel like because I've finally gotten out of my own way, I can enjoy my reputation. Because for all intents and purposes, what I should be right now is this never-do-well, embittered, unemployable guy arguing with some hooker outside a Malibu hotel scrambling for a syringe," he notes. "But I've got it really good. I've got a great gal, [and] my kid's good."[71]

Downney attends a Lakers game with his son, Indio. Downey's new, stable lifestyle enabled him to spend more time with his son.

The only thing missing from Downey's life—and the one thing that could cement his career resurgence—was a starring role in a blockbuster movie. As a successful producer, Susan Downey knew how important box office success could be for an actor's future prospects. She also realized that, despite his many gifts, her husband had yet to appear in a smash-hit film during his three-plus decade career in show business. As Downey's reputation steadily improved, he and his wife began looking for a mainstream film project that could launch him to the next level of stardom.

Chapter 6

Reaches the Top

In 2006, Susan Downey heard about a film project in the early stages of development that she felt would be perfect for her husband. Marvel Comics and Paramount Pictures were planning to make a live-action movie based on the comic-book superhero Iron Man. Iron Man was first introduced in print by the legendary comic-book writer Stan Lee in 1963. The secret identity of the powerful superhero, Tony Stark, is an arrogant playboy, genius inventor, and billionaire manufacturer of high-tech weapons. Stark becomes Iron Man after he is captured and held hostage by enemy forces armed with Stark Industries technology. He suffers life-threatening injuries and must wear an electromagnetic device to protect his damaged heart. Stark incorporates the device into an iron suit that makes him the ultimate weapon. After gaining his freedom, he becomes a superhero and uses the suit to fight evil.

The success of movie franchises based on other comic-book superheroes, like Batman and Spiderman, led to a great deal of interest in bringing Iron Man to the big screen. The project floated around Hollywood for years, with a variety of different writers, directors, actors, and production companies involved. When the movie rights finally reverted back to Marvel Comics in 2005, the publisher teamed up with Paramount to produce the film version of Iron Man. They hired writer/director Jon Favreau to oversee the project. After working with top comic-book writers to develop a screenplay, Favreau launched his search for an actor to play Tony Stark/Iron Man.

"I Am Iron Man"

As soon as Downey heard about the project, he became determined to win the role. "He really, really wanted it," Susan Downey recalls. "Other than Chaplin, it's the role he's gone after the hardest. He knew he could do it, and he knew he had to prove it to people."[72] Downey had always longed to be part of a blockbuster film franchise, and he believed that *Iron Man* held this potential. Now that he had entered his forties, Downey also realized that his window of opportunity for playing an action hero would soon close. In addition, he had been a fan of comic books since childhood.

First and foremost, however, Downey felt a deep, personal connection to the character of Tony Stark. He found many

For the 2008 film Iron Man *Downey played industrialist-turned-action-hero Tony Stark to rave reviews and huge box office success.*

parallels between his own experiences and the transformation Stark undergoes to become Iron Man. Downey asked:

Why am I the guy for this job? Because the story is the most duplicitous and conflicted of all the Marvel characters, because he's really just a guy who gets put in an extraordinary set of circumstances—partially due to his own character defects and partially due to his lineage—and you can pick a million Joseph Campbell myths and look them up, but none of them apply more to me, and there's nothing I could bring more to than this job and this story.[73]

Downey wanted the role so badly that he agreed to attend an audition for the first time since *Chaplin*. He spent the weeks leading up to the audition in intensive preparation. He worked out with weights and took protein supplements to add 20 pounds of muscle (9kg) to his frame. He not only practiced his lines but also wrote alternative dialogue and scenes to perform. Not surprisingly, Favreau was impressed by Downey's audition. "He was not the obvious choice, but my larger fear was making a mediocre movie; the landscape of the superhero is very picked over," he states. "I knew that Robert's performance would elevate the movie."[74]

Even though studio executives were pushing him to consider younger, lesser-known actors, the director became convinced that Downey's life experiences made him perfect for the role. "Tony Stark goes through a bit of a moral reawakening in this movie," Favreau explains. "You can't have a moral reawakening if you're in high school. You have to have done things in your life to be able to look back and say that I've made mistakes or maybe I should reevaluate the way I approach things."[75]

After winning the role he coveted, Downey continued to work hard throughout the filming. He found it particularly difficult to wear the Iron Man suit, which was hot, restricted his vision, and weighed 90 pounds (40.8kg). All of his hard work paid off when *Iron Man* hit theaters in the spring of 2008. The film received great reviews and became a huge success at the box office, taking in nearly $100 million in its opening weekend on its way to grossing more than $300 million in the United States

Stan Lee

Iron Man was originally created by comic-book legend Stan Lee. Lee was born as Stanley Lieber in New York City on December 28, 1922. In 1939, the teenager got a job as an office assistant at Timely Comics, which eventually became Marvel Comics. After paying his dues by filling ink pots and proofreading, he made his debut as a writer in a 1941 issue of *Captain America*.

Lee's most lasting contributions to the world of comics came in the late 1950s and the 1960s. When competitor DC Comics launched successful updates of several series based around superheroes, Lee responded by introducing a whole stable of popular new characters, including the Fantastic Four, the Hulk, Iron Man, Thor, the X-Men, and Spiderman. Lee's creations were unique in that they had physical and emotional flaws and dealt with real-world problems like substance abuse and racism.

In later years, Lee served as publisher of Marvel Comics and oversaw the expansion of the company into a media empire. He also dabbled in acting and made cameo appearances in *Iron Man* and several other movies based on his characters.

Stan Lee, the creator of the Iron Man character, as well as numerous other comic book superheroes, attends the premiere of Iron Man.

alone. Moviegoers and critics alike enjoyed *Iron Man*'s unique combination of drama, action, comedy, and heart. "Not only is it a *good* comic book movie (smart and stupid, stirring and silly, intimate and spectacular)," notes online reviewer Jim Emerson, "it's winning enough to engage even those who've never cared much for comic books or the movies they spawn."[76] By all accounts, Downey stole the show with his portrayal of Tony Stark. "Downey is at his charismatic best," Calvin Wilson writes in the *St. Louis Post-Dispatch*, "rendering believable Stark's transformation from self-indulgent jerk to socially conscious crusader."[77]

Downey was thrilled finally to have starred in a blockbuster movie after so many years as an actor—and so many highly publicized troubles offscreen. "I've never had it this good—this is my day in the sun—and I certainly don't want to look a gift horse in the molars,"[78] he stated. Many fans and Hollywood insiders also felt pleased to see Downey achieve the success he had long deserved. "To have another shot at this, after what he's had and lost, is as redemptive a story as the movie itself,"[79] said Favreau. "It's like the pit bull who's got his jaws on a chew toy. Nothing will take this away from him."[80]

Earns Another Oscar Nomination

While Downey was shooting *Iron Man*, actor/director Ben Stiller approached him about an intriguing new film project called *Tropic Thunder*. Stiller first came up with the premise for the film in the 1980s—a time when Hollywood churned out numerous movies set during the Vietnam War. Some of Stiller's actor friends went to U.S. military boot camps to prepare for their roles in these films. He started thinking about what would happen if a group of actors thought they were shooting a big-budget war movie but mistakenly got involved in an actual war. Stiller explored this theme in the dark comedy *Tropic Thunder*, which he wrote, directed, and costarred in.

Downey traveled to Hawaii to begin shooting *Tropic Thunder* just two weeks after he wrapped up *Iron Man*. He found it helpful to focus his creative energies on a new project. "Ben Stiller saved me from the ghastly fate of a crash after shooting *Iron Man*," he

In Tropic Thunder Downey received another Oscar nomination for playing a character in controversial blackface.

recalls. "The waiting around, the expectations, the not knowing how it was going to come out."[81]

Stiller asked Downey to play the role of Kirk Lazarus, a five-time Academy Award–winning Australian actor who takes his work very seriously. Lazarus and the other characters are sent out into the jungle to shoot a war movie. In the movie-within-the-movie, Lazarus portrays an African American soldier named Lincoln Osiris. Determined to make his portrayal as realistic as possible, Lazarus goes so far as to dye his skin to appear more authentically black. Shortly after Lazarus and the other actors begin their military training, they come under attack by a gang of drug smugglers. They convince themselves that it is all part of the movie, however, so they remain in character and fight.

Some people in the movie industry questioned Downey's decision to follow up the success of *Iron Man* by playing such an offbeat and potentially offensive role. After all, white actors wearing blackface makeup to play African Americans had been considered racially insensitive—and off-limits to Hollywood—for decades. Somehow, though, Downey managed to pull it off. He turned in a terrific performance that was both hilarious and subtle. "Whatever political spin people will want to put on it, the audacity of Downey's performance [is] the best reason to see the film," Todd McCarthy writes in *Variety*. "Always a brilliant mimic and quicksilver vocalist, Downey dons matted hair, beard, ghetto-spiked rasp and [blackface] makeup to play a grandly self-confident [actor] who will take no crap from anyone about his impersonation."[82] Downey found it ironic that he received his second Academy Award nomination—this time as Best Supporting Actor—for the controversial role. "It's so funny to me that the role is a guy who is an Oscar-seeking moron," he states. "His whole motivation is Oscars."[83]

Downey lined up his next major film project while he was on location shooting *Tropic Thunder*. British filmmaker Joe Wright "shows up in Hawaii, in the middle of the jungle, wearing a trilby hat," Downey recalls. "And he tells me this story about friendship and faith. All of a sudden I start feeling all my old theater heartstrings being pulled. Before Joe left the island, I knew I'd be doing *The Soloist*."[84] Downey played Steve Lopez, a newspaper columnist who discovers that a homeless man he meets on the streets of Los Angeles, Nathaniel Ayers, is actually a classically trained musician. As he tries to help Ayers find a place to live and reconnect with his musical talents, Lopez also raises awareness of the larger problem of homelessness. "*The Soloist* wouldn't work half as well without Mr. Downey's astringent, bristly take on a man whose best intentions eventually collide with difficult truths," reviewer Manohla Dargis writes in the *New York Times*. "The actor is a wonder."[85]

Launches a Second Action Franchise

Downey's remarkable string of hit movies continued with the release of *Sherlock Holmes* (2009), based on Sir Arthur Conan Doyle's famous series of novels about a brilliant British detective. Once again, Susan Downey learned about the project while it was in the early stages of development. Director Guy Ritchie planned to update the traditional detective story by turning Sherlock Holmes into a tough guy who competes in boxing matches and sword fights. Susan signed on as a producer and encouraged her husband to take on the role. "She said that when you read the description of the guy—quirky and kind of nuts—it could be a description of me," Downey notes. "When he feels he's not inspired or motivated by some creative charge, he'll fall into a state where he barely speaks a word for three days, and when he's engaged, he has incredible amounts of energy, superhuman energy."[86]

When the action-packed *Sherlock Holmes* was released on Christmas Day 2009, it broke the single-day box office record for the holiday by earning $25 million. It went on to reach the $100 million mark during its first week in theaters, making Downey the star of a second blockbuster movie franchise. Although the overall film received mixed reviews, many critics praised Downey's on-screen chemistry with Jude Law, who played Holmes's trusty sidekick, Dr. Watson. Downey also won a Golden Globe Award as Best Actor in a Comedy or Musical for his performance. "It seems impossible now that anybody other than Robert could have played him," says Ritchie. "He thinks like Sherlock Holmes, he's complicated like Sherlock Holmes, and he can really brawl."[87]

Shortly after he finished shooting *Sherlock Holmes*, Downey went back to work on a sequel to *Iron Man*. In *Iron Man 2* (2010), Tony Stark faces off against an evil Russian physicist (played by Mickey Rourke) and races against time to fix his failing electromagnetic heart device. Although the second installment in the franchise did not receive as favorable reviews as the first one, Downey's performance earned a great deal of praise. "It may seem counterproductive for any actor to attempt a full-

Sherlock Holmes (2009) broke the Christmas Day box office record and made Downey the star of a second blockbuster movie franchise.

scale performance in one of these wingding franchise movies, but Downey Jr. does it every time," notes Peter Rainer in the *Christian Science Monitor*. "It may be that he's one of those actors who is incapable of dumbing down for audiences. He gives you his best each time out."[88] Like its predecessor, *Iron Man 2* was a huge success at the box office, earning $133 million in its opening weekend.

Enjoys His Success

The two-year period between the release of *Iron Man* and *Iron Man 2* was by far the most successful of Downey's long career. "Thanks to a series of clever choices, Downey has pulled off one of the smartest second acts in recent showbiz history," Benjamin Svetkey writes in *Entertainment Weekly*. "After doing just about everything humanly possible to destroy a once-promising career—including spending the better part of a decade in courtrooms and even jail cells—he's finally fulfilling his potential. He's become a movie star."[89] Even Downey was surprised by the fact that every film project he became involved with after *Iron Man* seemed to turn into a major hit. "To tell you the truth, I haven't fully digested what's happened to me before, during, and after *Iron Man*," he admits. "But I do know that I don't want to waste any more time."[90]

As a proven box office draw, Downey had his choice of lucrative future projects. He agreed to star in a comedy called *Due Date* (2010) about an uptight man who must hitchhike across the country to see his child born. He also agreed to shoot a sequel to *Sherlock Holmes* that was expected to hit theaters in 2011. Finally, Downey signed on to play Tony Stark/Iron Man in a big-screen version of Marvel Comics' *The Avengers* (2012). In this film, Iron Man will become part of a team of superheroes that

Sherlock Holmes

Robert Downey Jr. jumped at the chance to portray one of the most famous characters in all of literature on the big screen. Sherlock Holmes was created by Scottish author Sir Arthur Conan Doyle in 1887. The fictional detective went on to appear in four novels and more than fifty short stories over the next four decades. Most of the tales are narrated by Holmes's trusted friend and sidekick, Dr. John Watson.

As presented in Doyle's stories, Holmes is a brilliant detective who is able to use keen observations and deductive reasoning to solve the most difficult cases. He is also described as eccentric in his habits and serious in his manner, with an arrogant sense of his own abilities. Holmes is a world-class expert in forensic chemistry, and he is also a formidable bare-knuckle boxer, sword fighter, and martial arts practitioner.

The enduring popularity of Sherlock Holmes has led to hundreds of adaptations of the stories on stage, screen, radio, and television over the years. Director Guy Ritchie chose to emphasize the character's tough side in his action-packed 2009 film version titled *Sherlock Holmes*.

also includes Captain America, the Hulk, Loki, Black Widow, Hawkeye, and Thor. Downey's family, friends, and many fans could not be happier to see him finally achieve superstardom. "People root for him," says longtime friend Joel Silver. "I mean, this is a guy who's been through such hell in his life—yes, a lot of it self-inflicted—but he's come out the other side. People want him to succeed."[91]

In 2009, Downey celebrated his success by purchasing a three-story, modern home in Venice, on the west side of Los Angeles. It features a rooftop swimming pool and a large office for him and his wife to share. It also has a bedroom for Indio and space for a new baby that the couple is hoping to add to their family. In many ways, Downey was as happy and contented as he had ever been—and he was determined not to take that for granted. "Life does what it does," he said in an interview with George Stephanopoulos for *Good Morning America.* "If you have a hold of any sort of moral psychology, and you have good support, and you're managing your position in society, it's so fragile. And it's such a beautiful thing to have that it's just worth holding on to."[92]

Downey's box office success has given him the freedom to pick and choose from among a variety of interesting acting projects. He looks forward to appearing in independent films or even making a return to the stage. "I definitely don't want to just go from one big franchise to another," he explained on *Good Morning America.* "I remember my roots. . . . Maybe I'll work my way back east and try something a little different."[93] Downey hopes that his newfound stardom might also give him the opportunity to pursue some professional goals outside of acting. For instance, he expressed some interest in following in his father's footsteps and moving behind the camera. "I think the best thing I could do for my soul and my own development would be to direct," he explains. "It's in my blood from my dad and it's [one of many] things I've always wanted to do that remain very, very much unrequited."[94]

Hagerstown - Jefferson
Township Lib

Introduction: From Hollywood Bad Boy to Box Office Superstar

1. Jim Emerson, "Iron Man," *Chicago Sun-Times*, May 2, 2008. http://rogerebert.suntimes.com/apps/pbcs.dll/article?AID=/20080502/REVIEWS/285399481.
2. Chip Kidd, "Robert Downey Jr.," *New York Times Magazine*, February 8, 2009, p. 45.
3. Ben Stiller, "The 2008 *Time* 100—Artists and Entertainers: Robert Downey Jr.," *Time*, April 30, 2009. www.time.com/time/specials/2007/article/0,28804,1733748_173 3752_1734629,00.html#ixzz0vl4k51ZN.
4. Quoted in Ben Falk, *Robert Downey Jr.: The Rise and Fall of the Comeback Kid*. London: Portico, 2010, p. 250.

Chapter 1: Born to Be an Actor

5. Quoted in Chris Nashawaty, "Marathon Man: After a Life Spent Trying to Outrun the Demons of Drug Addiction, Robert Downey Jr. Is Channeling His Energy Toward a New Slate of Films," *Entertainment Weekly*, October 28, 2005, p. 28.
6. Quoted in Scott Raab, "The Second Greatest Actor in the World: Robert Downey Jr.," *Esquire*, December 2009, p. 108.
7. Quoted in Jamie Diamond, "Robert Downey Jr. Is Chaplin (On Screen) and a Child (Off)," *New York Times*, December 20, 1992. www.nytimes.com/1992/12/20/movies/film-robert-downey-jr-is-chaplin-on-screen-and-a-child-off.html.
8. Quoted in Diamond, "Robert Downey Jr. Is Chaplin (On Screen) and a Child (Off)."
9. Quoted in Nashawaty, "Marathon Man," p. 28.
10. Quoted in Diamond, "Robert Downey Jr. Is Chaplin (On Screen) and a Child (Off)."
11. Quoted in Ana Figueroa and Julie Scelfo, "Robert Downey Jr. Takes It One Day at a Time," *Newsweek*, February 12, 2001, p. 52.

12. Quoted in Tom Gliatto, "Hitting Bottom: Sick, and Busted Three Times in Four Weeks, Robert Downey Jr. Becomes the Most Recent Casualty of Hollywood's Heroin Resurgence," *People Weekly*, August 19, 1996, p. 70.
13. Quoted in Kyle Smith, "Hitting Bottom: Robert Downey Jr. Makes Prison the Latest Stop in a Life of Misspent Promise," *People Weekly*, February 14, 2000, p. 135.
14. Quoted in Falk, *Robert Downey Jr.*, p. 23.
15. Quoted in Diamond, "Robert Downey Jr. Is Chaplin (On Screen) and a Child (Off)."
16. Quoted in Joan Juliet Buck, "An Exceptional Talent: After Dark Years of Addiction, Rehab, and Prison, Robert Downey Jr.," *Vogue*, April 2006, p. 370.
17. Quoted in Gliatto, "Hitting Bottom," p. 70.
18. Quoted in Raab, "The Second Greatest Actor in the World," p. 108.
19. Quoted in Buck, "An Exceptional Talent," p. 370.
20. Quoted in Buck, "An Exceptional Talent," p. 370.

Chapter 2: Emerges as a Rising Star

21. Quoted in Gliatto, "Hitting Bottom," p. 70.
22. Quoted in Lowri Williams, "Sarah Jessica Parker Knows All About Addiction . . . Thanks to Robert Downey Jr.," *EntertainmentWise*, March 16, 2006. www.entertainmentwise.com/news/14640/sarah-jessica-parker-knows-all.
23. David Denby, "More than Zero," *New York*, November 23, 1987, p. 104.
24. Quoted in Diamond, "Robert Downey Jr. Is Chaplin (On Screen) and a Child (Off)."
25. Quoted in Jon Wilde, "More than Skin Deep," *Guardian*, November 8, 2003. www.guardian.co.uk/film/2003/nov/08/features.
26. Quoted in Bernard Weintraub, "Sarah Jessica Parker on Stardom, Dating, and the Baby She'd Love to Have," *Redbook*, July 1, 1996, p. 54.
27. Quoted in Buck, "An Exceptional Talent," p. 370.
28. Quoted in Falk, *Robert Downey Jr.*, p. 72.

29. Vincent Canby, "Robert Downey Jr. in Charlie Chaplin Life Story," *New York Times*, December 25, 1992. http://movies.nytimes.com/movie/review?res=9E0CE5D7153CF936A157 51C1A964958260.
30. Jeffrey M. Anderson, "Resurrecting the Tramp," Combustible Celluloid. www.combustiblecelluloid.com/archive/chaplin92.shtml.
31. Quoted in Rebecca Winters Keegan, "Why Is This Man Smiling?" *Time*, April 28, 2008, p. 77.
32. Quoted in Keegan, "Why Is This Man Smiling?," p. 77.
33. Quoted in Buck, "An Exceptional Talent," p. 370.

Chapter 3: Caught in a Downward Spiral

34. Quoted in Steve Garbarino, "Robert Downey Jr.'s Last Party," *Detour,* February 1999. www.dandychick.com/rdjfilmguide/institute/rllp.php.
35. Stephen Holden, "The Last Party: About America as a Family That's Dysfunctional," *New York Times*, August 27, 1993. http://movies.nytimes.com/movie/review?res=9F0CEED614 39F934A1575BC0A965958260.
36. Todd McCarthy, "Short Cuts," *Variety*, September 7, 1993. www.variety.com/index.asp?layout=review&reviewid=VE1 117901214&categoryid=31&query=short+cuts&display= short+cuts&cs=1.
37. Janet Maslin, "A Yuppie Haunted (Really) by Other People's Problems," *New York Times*, August 13, 1993. http://movies .nytimes.com/movie/review?_r=2&res=9F0CE1DF1F38F9 30A2575BC0A965958260&partner=Rotten%20Tomatoes.
38. Quoted in James Lipton, "Inside the Actors Studio: Robert Downey Jr.," interview, July 9, 2006.
39. Quoted in Nashawaty, "Marathon Man," p. 28.
40. Jack Mathews, "Hugo Pool Doesn't Reflect Well on Downeys Jr. and Sr.," *Los Angeles Times*, December 12, 1997. www.calendar live.com/movies/reviews/cl-movie971230-7,0,4695421 .story.
41. Quoted in Garbarino, "Robert Downey Jr.'s Last Party."
42. Quoted in Falk, *Robert Downey Jr.*, p. 121.

43. Quoted in David Hochman, "Downey and Out in Beverly Hills," *Entertainment Weekly*, March 27, 1998, p. 34.

Chapter 4: Travels a Rough Road to Recovery

44. Quoted in Garbarino, "Robert Downey Jr.'s Last Party."
45. Janet Maslin, "Two Girls and a Guy: The Love Triangle as One-Man Show," *New York Times*, April 24, 1998. http://movies.nytimes.com/movie/review?res=9F07E2DF103FF937A15757C0A96E958260.
46. Quoted in Hochman, "Downey and Out in Beverly Hills," p. 34.
47. Quoted in Hochman, "Downey and Out in Beverly Hills," p. 34.
48. Quoted in Hochman, "Downey and Out in Beverly Hills," p. 34.
49. Quoted in Hochman, "Downey and Out in Beverly Hills," p. 34.
50. Quoted in Jeffrey Ressner, "From Hollywood to Hell and Back," *Time*, April 27, 1998, p. 66.
51. Quoted in Josh Rottenberg, "Extreme Holmes Makeover," *Entertainment Weekly*, November 27, 2009, p. 32.
52. Quoted in Falk, *Robert Downey Jr.*, p. 152.
53. Quoted in Ressner, "From Hollywood to Hell and Back," p. 66.
54. Quoted in Ressner, "From Hollywood to Hell and Back," p. 66.
55. Quoted in Falk, *Robert Downey Jr.*, p. 165.
56. Quoted in Wilde, "More than Skin Deep."
57. Quoted in Andrew Gumbel, "Downey Jr. May Never Act Again Following Dismissal from 'Ally McBeal,'" *Independent*, April 26, 2001. www.independent.co.uk/news/world/americas/downey-jr-may-never-act-again-after-dismissal-from-ally-mcbeal-682655.html.
58. Quoted in Smith, "Hitting Bottom," p. 135.

Chapter 5: Makes a Cautious Comeback

59. Quoted in Buck, "An Exceptional Talent," p. 370.
60. Quoted in Falk, *Robert Downey Jr.*, p. 155.

61. Quoted in Buck, "An Exceptional Talent," p. 370.
62. Quoted in Kevin West, "Mr. Clean: Married, Sober, and on the Road to Salvation, Robert Downey Jr. Pulls No Punches," *W*, March 2007, p. 392.
63. Quoted in *Entertainment Weekly*, "Free at Last," August 18, 2000, p. 16.
64. Quoted in Jason Lynch, "Back from the Edge," *People Weekly*, November 10, 2003, p. 85.
65. Quoted in Lynch, "Back from the Edge," p. 85.
66. Quoted in West, "Mr. Clean," p. 392.
67. Quoted in Natasha Stoynoff, "The Comeback Kid," *People Weekly*, May 19, 2008, p. 81.
68. Quoted in Hilary DeVries, "Robert Downey Jr.: The Album," *New York Times*, November 21, 2004. www.nytimes.com/2004/11/21/arts/music/21devr.html?pagewanted=1&_r=1&oref=slogin&adxnnlx=1210518255-AHT6ACtNjm%20MebN5u6Ef8g.
69. Benjamin Svetkey, "Entertainer of the Year: Robert Downey Jr.," *Entertainment Weekly*, November 21, 2008, p. 26.
70. Quoted in Svetkey, "Entertainer of the Year," p. 26.
71. Quoted in Nashawaty, "Marathon Man," p. 28.

Chapter 6: Reaches the Top

72. Quoted in Keegan, "Why Is This Man Smiling?," p. 77.
73. Quoted in Scott Raab, "The Quiet One: May God Bless and Keep Robert Downey Jr. and, If You're Up There, We're Not Kidding This Time," *Esquire*, March 2007, p. 149.
74. Quoted in David Carr, "Been Up, Been Down. Now? Super," *New York Times*, April 20, 2008, p. L1.
75. Quoted in Keegan, "Why Is This Man Smiling?," p. 77.
76. Emerson, "Iron Man."
77. Calvin Wilson, "Iron Man," *St. Louis Post-Dispatch*, May 2, 2008, p. GO40.
78. Quoted in Rottenberg, "Extreme Holmes Makeover," p. 32.
79. Quoted in Stoynoff, "The Comeback Kid," p. 81.
80. Quoted in Keegan, "Why Is This Man Smiling?," p. 77.
81. Quoted in Svetkey, "Entertainer of the Year," p. 26.

82. Todd McCarthy, "Tropic Thunder," *Variety*, July 25, 2008. www.variety.com/review/VE1117937830.html?category id=3359&cs=1.

83. Quoted in Wes D. Gehring, "Elementary, My Dear Downey," *USA Today* magazine, May 2009, p. 65.

84. Quoted in Svetkey, "Entertainer of the Year," p. 26.

85. Manohla Dargis, "*The Soloist:* Struggle and Rescue, a Duet in Sharps and Minors," *New York Times*, April 24, 2009. http://movies.nytimes.com/2009/04/24/movies/24solo.html.

86. Quoted in Falk, *Robert Downey Jr.*, p. 237.

87. Quoted in Rottenberg, "Extreme Holmes Makeover," p. 32.

88. Peter Rainer, "*Iron Man 2* Review," *Christian Science Monitor*, May 7, 2010. www.csmonitor.com/The-Culture/Movies/2010/0507/Iron-Man-2-review.

89. Svetkey, "Entertainer of the Year," p. 26.

90. Quoted in Svetkey, "Entertainer of the Year," p. 26.

91. Quoted in Rottenberg, "Extreme Holmes Makeover," p. 32.

92. Quoted in *Good Morning America*, "Robert Downey Jr. Is Iron Man," April 29, 2010. www.hulu.com/watch/145565/abc-good-morning-america-robert-downey-jr-is-iron-man.

93. Quoted in *Good Morning America*, "Robert Downey Jr. Is Iron Man."

94. Quoted in Raab, "The Second Greatest Actor in the World," p. 108.

1965
Robert Downey Jr. is born on April 4 in New York City.

1970
Downey makes his first film appearance in *Pound*, an experimental film directed by his father.

1973
Downey's parents allow him to try alcohol and marijuana.

1979
Following his parents' divorce, Downey moves to California to live with his father and attends Santa Monica High School.

1985
After playing supporting roles in several teen-oriented movies, Downey joins the cast of the late-night sketch-comedy TV series *Saturday Night Live*.

1987
Downey earns critical raves for his compelling portrayal of a drug addict in the film *Less than Zero*.

1992
Downey receives an Academy Award nomination for Best Actor for his portrayal of the legendary silent-film star Charlie Chaplin in *Chaplin*.

1995
Downey's substance abuse takes a turn for the worse when he begins smoking black-tar heroin.

1996
Following three arrests for drug-related offenses within a month's time, Downey is sent to a court-ordered rehabilitation facility.

1997
Downey suffers a relapse and is sentenced to four months in jail for violating the terms of his probation.

1999
When Downey falters once again in his recovery from drug addiction, he is sentenced to a year in prison.

2001
Shortly after winning a Golden Globe Award for his role on the TV series *Ally McBeal*, Downey is fired from the show for using drugs and spends a year in a court-ordered residential rehab program.

2002
Finally clean and sober, Downey meets producer Susan Levin on the set of the thriller *Gothika*.

2005
Downey marries Susan Levin on August 27.

2008
Downey stars as a comic-book superhero in the blockbuster movie *Iron Man*.

2009
Downey earns an Academy Award nomination for Best Supporting Actor for his role in *Tropic Thunder*; he also stars in *Sherlock Holmes*.

2010
Downey continues his superhero role as Tony Stark in *Iron Man 2*.

For More Information

Book

Ben Falk, *Robert Downey Jr.: The Rise and Fall of the Comeback Kid*. London: Portico, 2010. Written by a prominent entertainment journalist, this unauthorized biography examines Downey's formative experiences and their impact on his life and career.

Periodicals

Joan Juliet Buck, "An Exceptional Talent: After Dark Years of Addiction, Rehab, and Prison, Robert Downey Jr.," *Vogue*, April 2006. This feature article provides extensive information about Downey's childhood, early career, substance abuse, and recovery.

Rebecca Winters Keegan, "Why Is This Man Smiling?" *Time*, April 28, 2008. This in-depth profile, published following the box office triumph of *Iron Man*, looks back over Downey's early life and struggles with drug addiction.

Benjamin Svetkey, "Entertainer of the Year: Robert Downey Jr.," *Entertainment Weekly*, November 21, 2008. Naming Downey its Entertainer of the Year for 2008, *Entertainment Weekly* examines how the actor managed to pull off "one of the coolest comebacks ever."

Internet Sources

"Inside the Actors Studio: Robert Downey Jr.," interview, July 9, 2006. www.bravotv.com/inside-the-actors-studio/videos/robert-downey-jr-0. This clip from an episode of *Inside the Actors Studio* captures Downey discussing his preparation for the role of Chaplin.

"Robert Downey Jr. Biography," Biography.com. www.biography.com/articles/Robert-Downey-Jr.-9542052. This site offers a lengthy biography of Downey as well as clips from some of his major films.

Nathan Southern, "Robert Downey Jr.," *New York Times*, August 5, 2010. http://movies.nytimes.com/person/19966/Robert-Downey-Jr-/biography. This site provides a detailed overview of Downey's life and career.

Music Album

Robert Downey Jr., *The Futurist*. Arista Records, 2004. Downey's debut musical recording features nine original, introspective songs, along with a cover of Charlie Chaplin's "Smile."

Picture Credits

Cover: Jason Merritt/Getty Images Entertainment/Getty Images
AP Images/Carlos Jasso, 40
AP Images/Evan Agostini, 15
AP Images/Matt Sayles, 71
AP Images/Nick Ut, 43, 48, 58
Bob Peterson/Time Life Pictures/Getty Images, 12, 13
Carolco/Canal+/RCS Video/The Kobal Collection/The Picture Desk, Inc., 30
Dark Castle Entertainment/Columbia Pictures/Warner Bros./The Kobal Collection/Dory, Attila/The Picture Desk, Inc., 62
Dave Benett/Hulton Archive/Getty Images, 36
Dreamworks LLC/The Kobal Collection/Wallace, Merie W./The Picture Desk, Inc., 73
Fotos International/Archive Photos/Getty Images, 38
Icon Ent Int/Haft Entertainment/The Kobal Collection/The Picture Desk, Inc., 60
Jim Ruymen/UPI/Landov, 64
Jim Spellman/WireImage/Getty Images, 16
Kevin Winter/Getty Images, 33 Landov, 9
Lucy Nicholson/AFP/Getty Images, 54
Marvel Enterprises/The Kobal Collection/The Picture Desk, Inc., 69
MPI/Getty Images, 29
Noel Vasquez/Getty Images, 66
Online USA/Getty Images, 51
Paramount/The Kobal Collection/Conner, Frank/The Picture Desk, Inc., 50
Paramount/The Kobal Collection/Hamill, Brian/The Picture Desk, Inc., 22
Silver Pictures/The Kobal Collection/The Picture Desk, Inc., 76
20th Century Fox/The Kobal Collection/Clifford, John/The Picture Desk, Inc., 26
20th Century Fox/The Kobal Collection/The Picture Desk, Inc., 47
Universal/The Kobal Collection/Talamon, Bruce/The Picture Desk, Inc., 39
Universal/The Kobal Collection/The Picture Desk, Inc., 23

Laurie Collier Hillstrom is the author of more than twenty books, including previous volumes in the People in the News series on Al Gore, Dale Earnhardt Jr., and Jay-Z. She lives in Michigan with her husband, Kevin Hillstrom, and twin daughters, Allison and Lindsay.